T0194265

dry bones dancing

Tony Evans

Multnomah Books

DRY BONES DANCING
published by Multnomah Books
© 2005 by Tony Evans
International Standard Book Number: 978-1-60142-441-9

Cover design by David Carlson Design
Cover image by Tristan Paviot/Getty Images

Italics in Scripture quotations reflect the author's emphasis.
Unless otherwise indicated, Scripture quotations are from:
The Holy Bible, *English Standard Version*
© 2001 by Crossway Bibles, a division of Good News Publishers.
Used by permission. All rights reserved.

Published in the United States by WaterBrook Multnomah, an imprint of the
Crown Publishing Group, a division of Random House Inc., New York.

MULTNOMAH and its mountain colophon are registered trademarks
of Random House Inc.

For information:
MULTNOMAH BOOKS
12265 ORACLE BOULEVARD, SUITE 200
COLORADO SPRINGS, CO 80921

146655433

Contents

PART I

From Deadness to Dancing

PART II

Deepening Your Spiritual Passion

FrOm Deadness tO Dancing

DOWN
in the Valley

■ One day someone much like you or me paused long enough to look back on his life and land upon this realization:

First I was dying to finish high school and start college.
Then I was dying to finish college and start my career.
Then I was dying to get married and have children.
Then I was dying for my children to grow up and get out.
Then I was dying to retire.
And now, I'm just dying...and suddenly I realize I've for-
gotten to live.

Could that be the road you're driving down? Have you often found yourself waiting and hoping and looking for that "next thing" that could fill the vacuum in your life?

So many of God's people are like that. So many often feel stranded in a desert of hopelessness and emptiness. It's true today...and it was especially true at one particular moment in history that can teach us so much when we look back and reflect carefully upon it. In that moment, God's people were "dying" in the most tragic desperation conceivable.

But in their despair, God had a spiritual miracle to show them. And for your edification and mine, He has placed a record of that miracle in His Book. With the eyes of our hearts focused on that account, I want to quickly take you back with me to that amazing moment in that amazing place so that we can learn all we can.

I want to take us there to help us comprehend the degree of despondency His people were then experiencing (and into which we ourselves can often sink).

I want to take us there to discover how God invaded that place of despair in such a powerful and unforgettable way.

I want to take us there because the promise that almighty God announced on that occasion and in that location is for all His people for all time—and that means you and me, right now.

DISASTER AREA

It was a scene like nothing Hollywood ever imagined.

In fact, only the Spirit of God Himself could fully imagine it. And only in the Spirit of God could it be witnessed firsthand by any human being. That's exactly what happened to the prophet Ezekiel in the passage we're about to penetrate. So let's consider carefully every detail in the big picture God gave him.

> Only the Spirit of God Himself
> could fully imagine it.
>
> ■ ■ ■ ■ ■ ■ ■ ■ ■ ■ ■ ■ ■

"The hand of the LORD was upon me," the prophet tells us, "and he brought me out in the Spirit of the LORD" (Ezekiel 37:1). This was a supernatural encounter. It was a supernatural intervention into the life of a natural man. God's hand took hold of Ezekiel and lifted him above his everyday existence, outside his normal routine, and beyond his natural senses. What he experienced was a vision, yet because it came straight from the Spirit of God, it reflected a reality more real even than the physical reality we perceive around us.

God's hand carried off this man "in the Spirit." And what was their destination?

Ezekiel goes on to tell us exactly where he was taken and what he observed. He says that the Lord "set me down in the middle of the valley" (v. 1).

Ezekiel had been in such a place before. This same Hebrew word for "valley" is identical to the term used earlier in Ezekiel's book for a broad stretch of land where the Lord Himself had once instructed Ezekiel to go and meet Him (3:22–23; 8:4). On that occasion, when the prophet obeyed and went there in solitude, he saw in that place "the glory of the LORD" with such awesomeness that he fell to his face.

Perhaps in this new spiritual vision Ezekiel was transported to the very same expanse of land where he'd previously fallen to the ground in the presence of God's holy light. But if so, the sight now before him was something different in the extreme from his earlier encounter.

Ezekiel glanced all around him at this broad valley where the Lord had placed him and saw that "it was full of bones" (37:1). Not just piles of bones here and there, but a valley full of them.

Like a modern-day public official being flown in a helicopter over a disaster area, Ezekiel was given the full tour of this strange and gruesome sight. The Lord allowed him a careful inspection of this vast accumulation of human skeletal remains: "And he led me around among them, and behold, there were very many on the surface of the valley, and behold, they were very dry" (v. 2).

Not just several bones, but *very many.* Skulls and shoulder blades, kneecaps and ribs, femurs and vertebrae, hipbones and anklebones and fingerbones, all by the thousands.

And not just drab or stale, but *"very dry"*—as if they'd all been lying out there on public display, dead and exposed and baking in the hot sun for a long, long time.

God had a particular command to give Ezekiel in regard to these parched and brittle bones, and very shortly He would also provide him with a quite detailed explanation about them. But first God had a probing question to ask him, just as He sometimes has a few piercing questions for you and me to address before He's ready to reveal to us what He wants us to do or to know.

BIGGER THAN ME

Here was His question. The Lord God asked Ezekiel, "Son of man, can these bones live?" (37:3).

Ezekiel had just surveyed this vast and bizarre scene. He could not escape the conclusion that life and vitality were nonexistent in these bones. Bones, of course, are organic formations, developing only as part of some living creature; where there are bones, then of necessity there once was life. But in these dry relics filling the valley before Ezekiel's eyes, that life was long gone.

Could it be restored? Could there be life again where life had totally departed? Can strength and movement and energy and awareness and responsiveness somehow reappear in those who are so utterly dead that their bodies have decayed away, leaving nothing but bones—and even those very bones are disconnected and bleached and dry?

Is such a miracle possible?

God wanted to hear Ezekiel's answer, just as He sometimes wants us to carefully assess the true potential in whatever difficult situation lies before us. Perhaps we've concluded that a way out or a remedy or a resolution is impossible. Our condition or our circumstances seem hopeless. But is that really the case?

God was challenging Ezekiel to carefully evaluate the situation before him. He required a response, so of course Ezekiel gave Him one: "And I answered, 'O Lord GOD, you know'" (37:3).

When people say, "God only knows," it's the same as admitting that they themselves *don't* know. Ezekiel was no fool. He realized he didn't possess the answer to God's question. He was confessing, "Lord God, this is bigger than me. I myself cannot make these bones live again, and I don't know anyone else who can either. Only You know whether these bones could ever live again."

We so often offer to God our human assessment of the problem, along with our human solution to it. Ezekiel didn't do that. He wanted only God's assessment, and he wanted only God's solution.

"God, I don't know…but *You do*."

s such a miracle possible?

11

Ezekiel recognized impossibility when he saw it...but he did not forget that God is the God of the impossible.

Facing Up to Reality

Ezekiel must have sensed already who these bones represented. Even if he hadn't, God soon made the meaning clear: "Son of man, these bones are the whole house of Israel" (37:11).

So this was the devastating reality: God's people were nothing more than a valley-full of wretched bones, pathetic and passionless and useless. This was the accurate depiction of their spiritual condition. Like dry-roasted, disconnected skeletal fragments, and nothing more. Only bones that could not effectively walk or run or work. Bones that definitely were incapable of dancing and celebration.

That was the deepest reality among the people of God.

What would you and I see today if God were to grant us a personal vision of the true reality of our own spiritual condition? Or our family's spiritual condition? Our church's? Our nation's? What exactly would be in that picture? What would our valley be filled with?

Ezekiel didn't have to wonder. God gave him the clear image. And it showed that, spiritually speaking, God's people were missing something very critical—*life.* The "whole house of Israel" was this way, the entire nation. They were all dead and dry.

God's people were missing something very critical.

■ ■ ■ ■ ■ ■ ■ ■ ■ ■ ■

Their miserable inner condition was just as bleak as their outward circumstances. At this point in history, the Jews had been exiled from their homeland of Israel, and Jerusalem had recently been entirely destroyed. Ezekiel himself was in Babylon with his fellow captives. And in their captivity, they were suffering from an extreme case of spiritual emptiness and dryness and despair. God reminded His prophet of the people's cries and groans: "Behold, they say, 'Our bones are dried up, and our hope is lost; we are clean cut off'" (v. 11). Physically they felt inwardly drained of vitality because spiritually and mentally and emotionally they were without any hope.

They felt "cut off"—severed from life and vitality as well as from their sense of community. Each one felt inwardly disjointed, confused, and disconnected from one another. Their condition was perfectly captured in that vision of the valley of dry bones Ezekiel observed—for there's no one to go to for help when the person next to you is just as dead and dry as you are.

Spiritual dryness and dejection and disconnectedness had become a way of life for them. It was the norm—as it is so often with too many of us. And it hangs on for so long that we begin to lose hope of ever experiencing anything different.

But whenever this is true, God shows us how to change it. He's ready and eager to bring a new reality into existence for us.

ACTION TIME

For Ezekiel, in that valley of dried-up bones, the moment for action had come. God was going to perform a miracle, and He was going to use Ezekiel to accomplish it.

To bring about this miracle, God was simply going to speak His Word—His life-giving Word, His Word that is living and active and sharper than a two-edged sword, His Word that pierces deeply into our innermost delineation of soul and spirit and of joint and marrow and discerns there our hearts' every thought and motive (Hebrews 4:12).

And God was going to speak this Word through His prophet Ezekiel—"Prophesy over these bones," God commanded him, "and say to them, O dry bones, hear the word of the LORD" (37:4).

Then He gave Ezekiel a promise to announce for all God's people:

> "Thus says the Lord GOD to these bones: Behold, I will cause breath to enter you, and you shall live. And I will lay sinews upon you, and will cause flesh to come upon you, and cover you with skin, and put breath in you, and you shall live, and you shall know that I am the LORD." (vv. 5–6)

God was promising absolutely everything that these bones needed to become living, active beings. First and most importantly, He promised life-sustaining breath (notice how He mentioned it twice.) He also promised tendons, and He promised muscle, and He promised skin. These bones would be completely restored into living, breathing, active creatures, and more than that, they would be restored in their knowledge of the Lord God.

Now He was going to prove the answer.

■ ■ ■ ■ ■ ■ ■ ■ ■ ■ ■ ■

"Can these bones live?"—that's what God had asked Ezekiel. Now He was going to prove and demonstrate the answer.

Ezekiel did exactly what he was told. "So I prophesied as I was commanded" (v. 7). He spoke aloud to those bones and gave them God's message.

God was faithful to His promise. "And as I prophesied," Ezekiel says, "there was a sound, and behold, a rattling, and the bones came together, bone to its bone" (v. 7). These bones had been scattered and jumbled like puzzle pieces thrown in a box. But at God's command, every bone attached to another, linking to other bones exactly where it needed to. Where there'd been disconnection and chaos before, now there was order and shape and framework. It happened with a great sound, with countless clackings of bone to bone.

Ezekiel could now see full human skeletons, thousands of them, a valley full of them. Then more happened: "And I looked, and behold, there were sinews on them, and flesh had come upon them, and skin had covered them" (v. 8). From the *inside out* these skeletons were transformed into full-formed human bodies, all through the simple medium of God's Word. The bones took on tendons; the tendons took on muscle; the muscle took on skin.

STILL MISSING: LIFE

Yet something still was missing, as Ezekiel quickly noticed: "But there was no breath in them" (37:8).

God had promised breath...but as yet there was none. There was body and form, there was *potential* movement and action and responsiveness—but not yet actual life.

In this vision God was giving to Ezekiel and to us, He placed great emphasis upon life-giving breath. In the Hebrew way of thinking, the concepts of "breath" and "wind" and "spirit" are so closely linked that the same Hebrew word is used for all three. That word is *ruach,* and it's used four times in the sentence God spoke next to Ezekiel: "Prophesy to the breath; prophesy, son of man, and say to the breath, Thus says the Lord GOD: Come from the four winds, O breath, and breathe on these slain, that they may live" (v. 9).

Once again, the prophet obeyed: "So I prophesied as he commanded me…"

Once again, God was faithful to His Word: "…and the breath came into them, and they lived and stood on their feet, an exceedingly great army" (v. 10).

Where Ezekiel had seen before a valley filled with wasted, wretched bones, now he looked out upon the awesome sight of a vast and mighty host of living, breathing soldiers ready to do battle for the Lord.

POWER PROMISE

In that awesome moment for Ezekiel, God took the opportunity to preach His promise even more. He was sending the prophet back to speak again to the people, so at the close of this vision He gave him a powerful message to carry with him.

It was a promise all about *resurrection* and *restoration:*

"Therefore prophesy, and say to them, Thus says the Lord
GOD: Behold, I will open your graves and raise you from

your graves, O my people. And I will bring you into the land of Israel. And you shall know that I am the LORD, when I open your graves, and raise you from your graves, O my people." (37:12–13)

It was also a promise of true *life* from God's *Spirit:* "And I will put my Spirit within you, and you shall live" (v. 14).

And it was also a promise about *knowing* God and experiencing His *faithfulness:* "Then you shall know that I am the LORD; I have spoken, and I will do it, declares the LORD" (v. 14). In their day of despair, God was focusing their spiritual eyes on a brighter tomorrow when their relationship with Him would be better than ever: "When this thing is turned around, you'll have the true knowledge of God. When this thing is turned around, there'll be no doubt about who God is. When this thing is turned around, there'll be no question that there's only One who sits on the throne. You'll discover that I alone am your sufficiency to make dry bones live again and to keep them alive."

That's God's message for us as well. That's His good news for you and me. He has a supernatural turnaround awaiting us. He has a resurrection and a restoration and a spiritual renewal that will ultimately bring us more intimate knowledge of Himself.

When this thing is turned around, you'll have the true knowledge of God.

■ ■ ■ ■ ■ ■ ■ ■ ■ ■ ■ ■

Facing the Desperation

You may be despondent because dryness and passionlessness have become a way of life, and you're short on hope that it could ever change. You're dehydrating down in your valley, and your bones are sucked dry. There's been a severe loss of life—in your spirit or your mentality, or in your marriage or your family, or in your ministry or your church, or in some endeavor or concern that once was alive for you. But now the fire and the passion are gone.

Being honest, you have to admit to God, "Only You know whether this situation can be fixed. I don't have an answer, and if You're asking me how to make this thing live again, I have to say that only You know, because I have no clue."

As you face such desperation, the good news is that you don't have to give up. You don't have to run away. No matter how dry and hopeless you are, *these bones can live again.* These bones can thrive again. These bones can rejoice again. These bones can dance again because God is extending to you His promise of the Spirit's power, His promise of resurrection power, His promise of a great awakening. He's saying again, "I'll raise you from your grave."

A miracle is what you need, and a miracle is what He promises—a miracle of spiritual renewal in the place where all hope has been discarded.

A man in our community named Billy Trailor goes around to junkyards and construction sites and back alleys to look over stuff that other people have discarded as useless and good for nothing. Billy looks at that junk as an opportunity for a resurrection. He selects the discarded items he wants and takes them to his garage, where he carefully works to fashion them into objects of contemporary art. Some of them he has sold for thousands of dollars.

Something that was once perceived as being worth nothing can instead be put on display at a gallery—all because Billy turns trash into treasure. He creates miracles out of junk. He recognizes that the stuff others discard is really a miracle waiting to happen.

God has a miracle of renewal waiting to happen for you. Do you want to get ready for it? Do you want to know how to receive the spiritual renewal God promises?

That's what the rest of this book is all about.

THere's a ReasON
for This

When I was growing up, we spent a lot of Saturdays at the Lafayette Bowling Alley, which featured duckpin bowling—a game invented in my hometown of Baltimore. Duckpin bowling has smaller balls (weighing less than four pounds) and smaller pins (nine inches high instead of fifteen), which makes for quick throws and a more challenging game (unlike normal bowling, no one's ever scored a perfect game with duckpins).

In those days at Lafayette, they didn't have the sophisticated technology bowling alleys have today, and after a ball was thrown, the apparatus that was supposed to clear the knocked-down pins and set them up again for the next frame would always miss some. So they had a man there behind the wall at the end of the lanes whose job was to do what that device failed to accomplish. You would never see the man's face—only his feet, going from lane to lane, retrieving those knockdowns and standing them up again.

There's Someone whose face we can't see, Someone who's a specialist in going from life to life to life, picking up those who've been knocked down for a long time, then standing them up again after every other solution they've tried on their own has failed.

You know who I'm speaking of. And Ezekiel got a very dramatic picture of what this One can do on that day when he was taken to the valley of dry bones. Ezekiel saw how those who had collapsed to the ground in dry lifelessness were made to rise and stand on their feet as "an exceedingly great army." Almighty God Himself was the One who accomplished it.

Behind the Vision

Now let's step back a moment and consider the reason for this vision God gave Ezekiel. Seeing a valley full of dry bones naturally raises some questions: What caused this situation? What triggered the dryness? What created such lifelessness?

If you're seeking a cure, then normally you first identify the ailment; if you're looking for a solution, you first state the problem. So what was Israel's problem that brought the people to this appalling condition God portrayed so vividly in the valley for Ezekiel's eyes to witness? What caused those bones to fall there? What happened that made resurrection and restoration and renewal so necessary for God's people at that time?

Which leads naturally to a question about us today: When you or I experience extended times of dryness, what's the reason? What's the real cause of our lifelessness and lack of passion? Maybe, as we've tried everything we know to cure our lack of passion, we've been unsuccessful because we haven't addressed the true cause.

I f you're ongoingly dry, something is spiritually wrong.

■ ■ ■ ■ ■ ■ ■ ■ ■ ■ ■ ■ ■

So what is the actual problem?

Let me state the issue as emphatically as I can: If dryness is your normal spiritual state, then something's wrong in your life. We all have dry moments, of course. But if you're ongoingly dry, if you wake up to dryness daily, if you're living in dryness week after week, month after month, even year after year, if you're perpetually looking ahead for that next thing to give you a reason to live and to laugh and to celebrate…then something is spiritually wrong.

GOD'S GRIEF

In Ezekiel's situation, God had already informed him of the reason for Israel's dryness. To find the cause for their problem back then, all we have to do is turn back to the earlier pages in his book.

God told Ezekiel that His people had "defiled" the land of Israel "by their ways and their deeds" (36:17). He singled out two particular sins: "the blood that they had shed in the land" and "the idols with which they had defiled it" (v. 18).

Throughout the book of Ezekiel, idolatry was the sin God kept calling particular attention to. It was something that grieved Him deeply. He made this confession about Israel: "I have been broken over their whoring heart that has departed from me and over their eyes that go whoring after their idols" (6:9). He was so grieved because their idolatry brought a separation, a disconnection, a distance in their relationship with Him. He said the people's hearts "are all estranged from me through their idols" (14:5). And for God, this estrangement was painful. Something had to be done about it.

He reminded Ezekiel that even long ago, during the time when

He miraculously brought His people out of Egypt, "their heart went after their idols" (20:16). And their hearts had been at it ever since. Despite His constant warnings, they had never been cured of their idolatry. So out of His love and faithfulness, God had no choice but to discipline His people and remove them from the land of Israel. He knew that's what it would take to recapture their hearts and bring them close to Him again.

DISOBEDIENCE—DISTANCE—DRYNESS

It comes down to this: The reason the people were like a valley full of parched bones was that their disobedience had created distance, and distance had created dryness. They had rebelled against God and become estranged from Him. Now they were removed from fellowship with Him, and during this time of removal they inevitably dried up.

The same is true for us: Disobedience creates distance from God, and this distance creates dryness. If you're dry, it's because you're distant. And if you're distant, it's because you've been disobedient. Disobedience inevitably brings disconnection between us and God, and that disconnection always has a detrimental impact upon our spiritual life and passion.

Pluto, the ninth planet from the sun, is never a warm place to be. Pluto never heats up because it's so far from the sun. Distance has made it frigid and bleak, and it's that way every day of the year. Mercury, on the other hand, is blazing hot every day of the year, because it's so close to the sun. Distance to the sun directly affects temperature.

The same is true spiritually: Distance to the Son directly affects temperature, and far too many of us are satisfied with a long-distance relationship with our Lord. Some Christians are Pluto saints; they're in the orbit, but that orbit is so remote, so far from the center, that their spiritual life is always cold. But others are Mercury saints, always staying close to the Son so that they're constantly aflame, and the rest of us wonder what's wrong with them! Nobody's supposed to be hot *all* the time.

Spiritually speaking, most of us don't live on Pluto, and most of us don't live on Mercury. Most of us live on Earth where it's sometimes hot and sometimes cold. We're on again, off again in our spiritual condition. We're neither consistently up nor consistently down, but always in fluctuation. Sometimes we're ablaze with passion; sometimes we're as cold as ice.

And it's all about distance.

In the Bible, dancing is frequently associated with celebration and rejoicing. God intends for your spirit to dance; He intends for spiritual rejoicing to be the norm in your life and for dryness to be the exception. But if there's little celebration on the inside—if dryness is normal, and dancing is the exception—it's because there's been distance between you and God, and what caused that distance is disobedience.

It's all about distance.

■ ■ ■ ■ ■ ■ ■ ■ ■ ■ ■ ■

The Right Diagnosis

Perhaps you're thinking that even though there's an element of dryness in your life (maybe even a lot of dryness), disobedience definitely can*not* be the problem. Because you're aware that God has blessed you with so much, and you're enjoying those blessings. And you're not highly aware of any specific disobedience. In fact, you're not even comfortable with exploring that line of thinking.

But you may be like one of the churches in the book of Revelation with whom Jesus had to have a very candid talk. He gave it to them straight: "For you say, I am rich, I have prospered, and I need nothing, not realizing that you are wretched, pitiable, poor, blind, and naked" (3:17).

These people had totally misdiagnosed their situation, and it led to a gravely mistaken complacency. Externally they looked okay. They could say, "We've got the money in the bank, a nice house in a nice neighborhood, two cars. We're all right. We're doing just fine."

But God tells them, "You haven't been consulting with the right doctor."

You see, apparent external blessing does not necessarily mean internal spirituality. Just because you prayed and fasted for a new car and got it, or a new house and got it, or a new job and got it, doesn't mean you're spiritually on target. That's the danger of wanting to be blessed externally but not wanting to be dealt with internally.

Jesus told these people the truth: They were in a bad situation—wretched and miserable, in fact. He was saying, "Your self-assessment cannot be trusted. When I look at your x-ray, what I see is far worse than you realize." They were looking at themselves through the wrong glasses, and not through the "Son glasses" that Jesus alone could provide them.

Which reminds me of the couple who drove their car into a service station. The husband, sitting behind the wheel, asked the attendant to clean the windshield. So the attendant cleaned it while filling the car with gasoline. When the tank was full, he stepped to the driver's window to receive payment.

"I thought I asked you to clean the windshield," the driver said.

"I did, sir," the attendant replied.

"But look at it. It's filthy!"

"Sir," the attendant said, "I'd be glad to do it again." So he cleaned it again.

The driver was more irritated than ever. "Why can't you get it clean?" he demanded.

Then his wife said, "Honey, look at me." He leaned her direction. She took his glasses off, took out a tissue and wiped them off, and gave them back. He put them on, and the windshield was spotless.

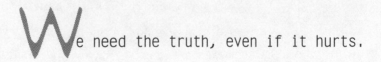

We need the truth, even if it hurts.

The lenses through which you're evaluating your life may be too dirty to give you the true picture. So let Jesus make the evaluation for you. His words may seem harsh, but only because of the faithfulness of His love. He tells us, "Those whom I love, I reprove and discipline, so be zealous and repent" (Revelation 3:19). His reason for telling us that we're wretched, miserable, poor, blind, and naked is simple—He loves us. And we should want nothing less from Him. If we've got cancer, we don't want the doctor telling us just to go home and take two aspirin and rest, and we'll be fine. It doesn't help us any when our problem is bigger than the remedy. We need the truth, even if it hurts. We need His true correction at our true point of need. And when He gives it (as He always does), it's fresh evidence that He still loves us.

THERE'S IDOLATRY SOMEWHERE

Distance and dryness took hold of Israel because of their idolatry—God made that clear to Ezekiel. And here's the strange thing: Israel kept up their sacrifices in the temple of the Lord even while they were secretly worshiping idols. All the while doing the religious thing for God—yet turning their hearts after false gods.

But maybe we shouldn't be so surprised. Have you ever wondered how today we can have all our church services, all our Christian conferences and concerts and seminars, all our Christian books and CDs, all our Christian radio and TV programs—yet still so many of us are so dry? How can we go to church every Sunday and read our Bible verse every day, yet stay so spiritually flat?

It's because there's an idol somewhere.

What is an idol? An idol is anything you try to put in God's place in your life. Idolatry is when you're looking in any other direction besides God in order to get what only God can give you. Idolatry means you're trying to orbit yourself around something else in addition to God, and that never works, just as Jesus warned us: "No one can serve two masters" (Matthew 6:24).

Idolatry is not just bowing down to some graven image. To be an idolater, you don't have to worship a rock or a tree. You can worship the paper that comes from the tree, the paper called money.

And so often the situation compounds itself. Even a small amount of idolatry in our lives will start to bring distance and dryness. It dehydrates our soul and takes away our spiritual celebration. So we look to something or someone else to alleviate that emptiness. But whatever it is we look to simply becomes another idol, so the crisis only deepens. We keep looking to other sources—other people, or more possessions, or a certain position with more prestige or more power—to obtain what God alone can provide. We keep turning desperately to somebody or something else to meet our increasing needs and to solve our intensifying problems and to repair our worsening situation.

MISDIRECTED FIRST LOVE

Idolatry means giving to something or someone else the "first love" that belongs only to the Lord.

In the book of Revelation, Jesus had to tell a certain church that they'd left their first love (2:4). The people in this church were plenty religious enough; Jesus commended them for their hard work and their steadfast perseverance and their doctrinal correctness. They served the Lord and sacrificed for Him and even suffered for Him. But He had a problem with them: Their external performance was impeccable, but they had a heart problem. He was saying, "When I put the stethoscope to evaluate your heart, we've got something missing." And what was missing was their first love. They had a relationship deficit because they had abandoned their first love.

What that tells you and me is that it's possible to be religious and yet not be enjoying a relationship with God. It's a love thing, but we so easily forget that religion does not equal relationship. We don't have a religion problem, we have a relationship problem.

It's not that we don't love the Lord at all, but that we no longer love Him first. When He first saved us, He was all we had. But then we get so occupied, so distracted by good stuff (not bad stuff), that our first love goes elsewhere than to God.

What is "first love"? How do you distinguish it from second love, third love, fourth love, and so on?

Foremost, it involves priority. *First* means first—it comes before anything else. Another ingredient—just as important—is passion. First love is more than functional love; it's *fiery* love.

It's like the passion between a man and woman who are newly in love. They don't need a manual on how to pursue their relationship; when the fire is there, fire *is* the manual. Only when the fire goes out do you feel the need to look for a manual or some program.

And when it happens in a marriage that a couple's first love is lost, then what they need is not a vacation, or a weekend away, or an exchange of expensive gifts. That's merely a program, and when the program is completed, they're right back where they started. No, what they need is the same thing the Lord wants, and that's first love. That's why so many couples were happier years ago in their cramped little apartments than they are now in their big houses. They've got the program down, but there's no fire. No burning.

When the fire is there, fire is the manual.

■ ■ ■ ■ ■ ■ ■ ■ ■ ■ ■ ■

Keep Serving

Now, don't misunderstand. When Jesus commended this church for faithful work and service but then went on to fault them for losing their first love, He wasn't suggesting that they stop those other things. He was saying, "Don't let your performance get in the way of relationship. Instead, let it grow out of relationship." Don't let the hard work you're doing for someone replace the Someone you're doing it for.

I was passing through the Atlanta airport one day on my way back to Dallas when I discovered that a famous soul food restaurant in Atlanta had opened a location in the airport. They make some of the best fried chicken I've ever tasted, and I can hardly describe how much I like it. So I looked at my watch and determined that I had plenty of time to enjoy some of that chicken while I was waiting to board Flight 74 to Dallas.

I got in the line and ordered three chicken thighs and a biscuit and then sat down to eat my delicious hot meal. Just as I took my seat, I happened to hear the loud speaker announce the last call for Flight 74 to Dallas.

I was in a dilemma. The flight was calling to me, but so was the chicken. Obviously I didn't come to the airport to eat chicken; I came to catch flight 74 from Atlanta to Dallas. The meal was only incidental to my being there, not the reason for being there. I sat there a few moments weighing what to do. Eat the chicken and risk missing my flight? Or catch the flight and leave my chicken?

I'll tell you what I did. I took my chicken with me on the flight.

God isn't asking you to give up the "chicken" of the service you have been faithfully giving Him. He's just saying, "Don't miss the flight of first love." He expects you to sacrifice for Him. He expects you to be steadfast. He expects you to stay doctrinally true. He even expects you to suffer for Him. But He doesn't expect you to miss the plane. Because He married you for a *relationship,* not for your service. And God would rather have a relationship with you in a cramped apartment than have an empty, stale cohabitation with you in a big house.

God saved you first and foremost for a love affair. He saved you to allow you to fall in love with Him. And that's why when we forget, obeying Him is often a big problem. Because Jesus says, "If you love me, you will keep my commandments" (John 14:15). Why is keeping His commandments so difficult for us so often? Because we don't love Him enough. He tells us that our true love will naturally produce obedience. The inspiration will be there; the motivation will be there. So when we try to produce obedience when there's a lack of love, it gets hard fast. But when the love is there, the duty easily follows.

The apostle John tells us, "For this is the love of God, that we keep his commandments. And his commandments are not burdensome" (1 John 5:3). Religion is weighty, but when love is there, there's no sense of burden. Yes, they are commandments to obey; yes, there's work to do; yes, He has expectations of us. But when you understand them in the context of your relationship with Jesus, you'll enjoy your obligations rather than be weighed down by them. You'll understand what Jesus meant when He said, "My yoke is easy, and my burden is light" (Matthew 11:30).

We want to get close enough to be drenched by His glory.

■ ■ ■ ■ ■ ■ ■ ■ ■ ■ ■

CLOSE UP AND DRENCHED

On one of our vacations, we visited Niagara Falls. When we arrived at our hotel, I got my first sight of the falls. I looked out and said, "Wow!" I was genuinely impressed. It was magnificent.

The next morning after breakfast we went down to a park near the falls, close enough that every now and then we could feel mist carried by the breeze from the crashing waters, and the roar was thunderous. And I said, "Glory!" From this close, the waterfall was a glorious sight.

But there's another way you can see the falls. It's called the Maid of the Mist. The Maid of the Mist is a boat that approaches the falls from the river below. When you board the Maid of the Mist, they give you a raincoat and an umbrella, because you get drenched from the spray. That's how close it gets.

Some of us are looking at Jesus only from the distant hotel room window of our lives; we're duly impressed, but not impacted. Others of us move closer to see Jesus from a nearby park, and every now and then we feel the mist of His presence. But a few of us aren't satisfied with either the hotel room or the park. We want to board the Maid of the Mist and get close enough to be drenched by His glory, drenched by His presence, drenched by His power, drenched by His purity—and as far away from dryness as we can possibly be. And that's exactly the kind of first-love relationship He wants us to have with Him.

Getting Specific

Are you consistently dry?

I'm not talking about consistently facing tough circumstances and difficult trials. That was frequently the case for Paul, but he wasn't spiritually dry. When Paul was suffering in prison, he wrote, "Rejoice in the Lord always; again I will say, Rejoice" (Philippians 4:4). He could say that because he lived that way himself. His external condition might not have been happy, but internally, in his spirit, he was moist, not dry.

Are you tired of being spiritually tired? Do you feel that your spiritual vitality has been ebbing away for a long, long time? Have you wondered at times how much longer you can go on like this?

Then think with me again about what I've been saying: Distance is the reason for the dryness, and disobedience is responsible for the distance.

Now, you may not like that fact. You can ignore it. You can decide not to pay any attention to it. But that won't make you less dry.

So are you willing to see yourself, apart from God's miracle, as nothing more than a pile of bones, spiritually speaking? Are you willing to accept that your dryness has been caused by a distance, which has come about because of disobedience?

I can't show you exactly what your specific disobedience is; it could be any of a million different things that can tempt us as an idol. I can't pinpoint exactly which one it is in your life; the Holy Spirit has to show you that.

All I can give you in this book are the underlying truths and essential principles and ask you to pray, "Holy Spirit, as I read through these pages, give me the specific application for me. I need to hear Your voice. Show me what You want me to do."

Let me assure you that God is deeply concerned that you identify and be cleansed from that disobedience and then be restored to a proper relationship with Him. He's deeply committed to bringing new life into your dry bones.

And He knows exactly how to do it.

When the spirit's wind Blows

■ When it really comes down to it, how can dried up bones be brought to life again? How exactly does God do that? What's His process?

It's a lot like popcorn. First you put the bag in the microwave. Inside the bag are kernels of corn, each one with a hard outer shell. But inside every kernel, there's moisture. As the microwave heats the kernels, the moisture heats up and becomes steam. The steam expands, pressing against the shell.

And you know what happens next:

Pop.

Pop.

Pop-pop.

Pop-pop-pop.

Poppoppoppoppoppoppoppoppoppoppopp...

It happens from the inside out. The living pressure inside is more than that hard outside can take, and the whole thing explodes into something new.

That's what God's spiritual renewal is like.

SOMETHING NEW

I mentioned earlier how God had previously informed Ezekiel what Israel's root problem was, even before He showed him the valley of dry bones. Just by reading the earlier pages in Ezekiel's book, we find out plenty about the reason for Israel's dryness and deadness.

That's where we also discover more about God's plan for a miracle of new life. God had been promising Ezekiel that He would bring about a supernatural rebirth in His people's hearts. He promised to replace their hard and stony hearts with "a new heart, and a new spirit"; He promised to put His very own Spirit within them so they would truly obey Him as His very own people (11:19–20; 36:25–27).

That's why God pleaded fervently with Israel to repent and throw off their disobedience and discover life: "Cast away from you all the transgressions that you have committed, and make yourselves a new heart and a new spirit! Why will you die, O house of Israel? For I have no pleasure in the death of anyone, declares the Lord GOD; so turn, and live" (18:31–32).

What was behind this "new heart" and "new spirit"?

Two words: *New Covenant.* God was promising all the enablement and motivation His people needed to live in obedience to His ways. That was His new promise and agreement for Israel…and through the blood of Christ, it's His new promise and agreement for you and me as well (Jeremiah 31:31–34; Matthew 26:28; Hebrews 8:7–13; 12:24).

How does this New Covenant work?

Two words again: *Word* and *Spirit.*

T he only words that will work for a cure
are divine words.

■ ■ ■ ■ ■ ■ ■ ■ ■ ■ ■ ■

There in that valley, God first commanded Ezekiel to "prophesy over these bones" (37:4). Which means Ezekiel was to declare the Word of God to them. He wasn't to take those bones to a doctor or a psychiatrist or a spiritual medium. Those bones were spiritually barren and dry, and only spiritual words could medicate the situation. When disobedience leads to distance resulting in dryness, the only words that will work for a cure are divine words.

So Ezekiel spoke the Word of the Lord, and there was sound and there was movement among those bones, as bone attached to bone. By the power of the Word of God, that which was unconnected became connected. By the power of His Word, scattered bones became skeletons, which then became covered in sinew and flesh and skin. Fragments became a framework, and the framework took on completed shape and form, all from the inside out.

It Takes More than the Bible

But there was a problem. The bones had become complete bodies, but the lungs inside were empty and still. There was no breath, no life. Before those bodies were finally able to stand up as living, breathing soldiers of God, Ezekiel first had to obey that next command from God: "Prophesy to the breath [Hebrew *ruach*]." When he did, "the breath [*ruach*] came into them, and they lived" (37:9–10).

What did all this mean? God quickly explained it by making this promise to Israel: "I will put my Spirit [*ruach*] within you, and you shall live" (v. 14).

It reminds us of how God created Adam: "The LORD God formed the man of dust from the ground"; but it was only when God "breathed into his nostrils the breath of life" that Adam "became a living creature" (Genesis 2:7).

And here's the lesson for us: It takes more than hearing and receiving God's Word to remove the spiritual dryness from our lives. You can hear the Bible preached all day long and still remain essentially lifeless. You can jump up and shout and sing, "I looked at my feet and my feet looked new; I looked at my hands and they did too." But the Bible by itself can only make the connections; it can't give you the breath. Without the Spirit's breath of life, you're still very much like a corpse, spiritually speaking.

Being under the Bible is fundamental, but not sufficient. Hearing the Bible preached is absolutely necessary, but not enough. Memorizing verses is critical, but it won't change you. Going to church, listening to Christian radio, reading Christian books—all this is wonderful, but you can do it all and still be spiritually inert and unresponsive. In order to rise up and stand and march out of that dry valley, we've got to first have life, not just connection and form.

If you're ongoingly dry and there's no life in you, it's either because the Spirit of God isn't in you (and you're not actually a Christian), or because He's in you but not at work because you aren't living under the Holy Spirit's control.

What makes the difference between a Christian who's actually advancing and one who's like a runner on a treadmill—lots of effort and activity, but no forward progress? The missing ingredient is the Holy Spirit. No Christian has more of the *presence* of the Holy Spirit than another Christian; however some Christians have more of the *power* of the Holy Spirit than other Christians.

The Holy Spirit's job is to make you alive, and only the Holy Spirit can do it.

■ ■ ■ ■ ■ ■ ■ ■ ■ ■ ■

ONLY SOURCE OF LIFE

"The Spirit gives life" (2 Corinthians 3:6). The Holy Spirit's job is to make you alive, and only the Holy Spirit can do it. A teacher can motivate and inspire you, he can make you laugh or cry, he can help you mentally understand, but he cannot give you life. Only the Spirit can do that—and God's promise in the New Covenant is that He *will* do it. And when the Spirit gives life, all the dryness is gone, because the Spirit causes "rivers of living water" to flow from our hearts (John 7:38–39).

Jesus said He came that we "may have life and have it abundantly" (John 10:10). He came to give us life—as our Savior—and to give abundantly—through the New Covenant.

If you not only hear God's Word, but also apply it by submitting to the Holy Spirit, based on the promise of God, no matter how dry and lifeless your spiritual experience has been or is now, you'll be able to live again and rejoice again and dance again. You'll know *personally* the truth spoken by Nehemiah: "The joy of the LORD is your strength" (Nehemiah 8:10).

God's New Covenant works because it brings a change in inner motivation, all by the Holy Spirit's power. In the New Covenant, God promises to write His laws on our minds and hearts (Jeremiah 31:33; Hebrews 8:10). It's like we've been placed on His spiritual photocopier, and His Word has been permanently imprinted onto our hearts.

And because God's Word inside us is "living and active" (Hebrews 4:12), it brings us a new disposition. We have the ability to obey God not because we have to, but because in our innermost being we truly want to. That's the kind of dynamic relationship with us that God wants, and the Holy Spirit makes it a reality. He connects us with God's life so we can have His life operating within us.

The Old Covenant, "the Law," was written on stone and was driven by external performance. The New Covenant, "the covenant of grace," is the covenant of the Spirit and is written on the heart. It has to do with internal enablement rather than merely external performance.

WE CAN'T DO IT

There's a reason the Holy Spirit is called the *helper.* God fully understands that you can't pull off what He expects. God goes into this knowing that you are a failure, and so am I. He goes into this knowing that His standards are way up here and we're way down here. He knows that our best efforts won't get us very high, and even if we get there we won't stay there too long. And so God, knowing of our insufficiency, has granted us a new power source, the Holy Spirit, whose job it is to enable Christians to live kingdom lives.

I'm learning more than ever that it's "not by might, nor by power, but by my Spirit, says the LORD of hosts" (Zechariah 4:6). Waiting on the Spirit can be irritating, frustrating, intimidating. Waiting for this supernatural endowment can be a little weird because we're so used to doing it ourselves—especially in America. And there's lots we can do by ourselves, but after we finish whatever we're doing, we wind up only with cheap imitations of what heaven can do.

And here's a particular danger we face in our evangelical culture, because we emphasize the Bible and objective truth so much: We can conclude that merely because I study it, believe it, and know it, I got it. Nothing could be further from the truth. In your pursuit of God, in your desire for spiritual passion, the Holy Spirit's active involvement is indispensable. He's not a negotiable item. And all of our accumulated information becomes only dead orthodoxy without the Spirit. Yet it's also true that the Spirit without information becomes empty sentimentalism. That's why it always takes both the Spirit *and* truth to make life work.

Getting Above

So what will happen when we actively yield to the Spirit's control?

There's no better place to go for an answer than the book of Acts. Before Jesus ascended into the clouds, He gave a promise that echoed what Ezekiel heard from God back in the valley of dry bones: "You will receive power when the Holy Spirit has come upon you" (1:8).

Recall with me how that promise was fulfilled on the day of Pentecost, when the Holy Spirit came down upon the first Christians: "And suddenly there came from heaven a sound like a mighty rushing wind" (Acts 2:2). This blast of wind came all of a sudden—out of nowhere God showed up. I like that word *suddenly* because it means I may not see ahead of time what the Spirit is up to; I won't be able to predict what He'll do and how He'll do it. *Suddenly* means I may not foresee His activity.

And this Spirit-blast "came from heaven." It was a solution different from anything mere human beings could supply because it came from a different source—from above, from out of this world. On our own, all we have access to are earthly things, earthly people, earthly resources, earthly strategies. We have earth at our disposal, but what the Holy Spirit brings is a *heavenly* something. And if we're going to pull off all that we know the Lord calls us to do, we're going to need a power greater than ourselves to do it.

So often we get trapped in despair and hopelessness because we're bound by earthly perspectives. For example, if you and your wife or husband are considering a divorce, there's something I can guarantee about your thinking: I can guarantee that the two of you together haven't yet learned to live in God's presence and to see your relationship from His higher perspective. Your thinking is

What the Holy Spirit brings is a heavenly something.

■ ■ ■ ■ ■ ■ ■ ■ ■ ■ ■ ■ ■

limited. It's bogged down in earthly perceptions—such as, "Our personalities are so different." Of course they're different. They always have been. They were different when you first met each other, and they were different while you were dating. You just covered them up back then.

But, you say, "Our differences are irreconcilable." Let me tell you something: Whenever two sinners are living in the same house, you're always going to have irreconcilable differences. You're going to have incompatibilities all over the place, everywhere you turn. It comes with the territory. That's reality.

But that's not your problem. Your problem is that you haven't learned to see the heavenly perspectives and the heavenly realities that supercede and override the earthly realities. You're still earthbound in your thinking. You're not truly pursuing God together with your husband or wife; you're stuck in your own narrow, self-focused, earthbound pursuits.

Or maybe you're thinking, "But a failing marriage is not my problem; my trouble's worse than that. My problem's bigger than that." Whatever your difficulty is, I know one thing about it: It's an earthly problem. It's an earthly situation. You may think it's insurmountable, but it's insurmountable only as long as your perspective stays on ground level. What you need is the mighty wind of the Spirit to blow heavenly realities and heavenly perspectives into your life and your heart and your mind.

NEEDING A HURRICANE

By the way, when it comes to wind and breath and spirit, the Greek language of the original New Testament is a lot like the Hebrew of the Old Testament—the same basic word can be used for all three concepts. We noticed that earlier with the Hebrew word *ruach*; in Greek, the word is *pneuma*.

We see this played out, for example, in the words Jesus spoke to Nicodemus: "The wind blows where it wishes, and you hear its sound, but you do not know where it comes from or where it goes. So it is with everyone who is born of the Spirit" (John 3:8). The same basic word is used for both "wind" at the beginning of that verse and "Spirit" at the end. And it reinforces for us the image of how the Spirit blows vitality and power into our lives.

Sometimes, of course, the wind may blow like a gentle breeze that you barely feel. Other times it's a blast that nearly knocks you over. That's what it was on the day of Pentecost. The gust of the Spirit sounded like a "mighty rushing wind" that "filled the entire house where they were sitting" (Acts 2:2). It was a windstorm out of nowhere, and the place was consumed with it.

We need a hurricane. We need a typhoon, a tornado.

That's the kind of contact we need with the Spirit today. For many of the issues and challenges we're dealing with in our individual lives and our families and our churches and our nation, we need a hurricane. We need a typhoon, a tornado. We need a blast of the Spirit that knocks us around, not just a mere puff to kiss our cheek. Ordinary stuff just won't do.

Maybe you feel that way already about your life. You're saying,

"If I don't get a miracle, if I don't get this God-coming-out-of-nowhere stuff, I can't even imagine how I'll make it." If so, you're a perfect candidate for the wind of the Holy Spirit.

There are a lot of Christians for whom it's been a long time since the Holy Ghost blew fresh life into their routine. They have to admit that there's been very little new experience of God for them lately. They can't tell you the last time there was a "mighty rushing wind" that suddenly blew the Spirit's energy into their existence. They can't tell you the last time Heaven came out of nowhere and addressed their need. Why? Mostly because they've been stuck in do-it-yourself Christianity. They've become so self-sufficient that God doesn't even have an opportunity to show them He's God. They're too busy for that.

And they're missing out on so much.

THE UPDRAFT OF THE SPIRIT

When God showed up on the day of Pentecost and those first believers in that place were filled with the Spirit, they could immediately do supernatural things that they could never have learned to do on their own, even in a lifetime. They immediately began to experience life at a much higher level.

Why? Because the filling of the Spirit means that you come under God's supernatural control and you act *outside your natural self*. It means experiencing what I call the updraft of the Spirit.

The Spirit's updraft blew from higher than ground earth, so that throughout the rest of the book of Acts these people were living and speaking no longer as mere human beings, but took on heavenly characteristics. They took on heavenly power and heavenly capability. And it was obvious to everyone around them.

In the Bible, the filling of the Spirit is never an invisible thing in its results and its impact and its effect. How do we know that? Because the Bible mentions the filling of the Spirit as a criteria, and that would be impossible if its effects were invisible. A little later in the book of Acts, when it came time to choose the first deacons, the church was instructed to choose men who were "full of the Spirit" (6:3). Which means that the filling of the Spirit has to be an observable commodity.

So what makes it observable? What does the filling of the Spirit look like?

It shows up as people who are acting outside themselves. People who don't live on the level of the earth but on the level of heaven, even though they're functionally and physically located on earth. Earth doesn't control their activity and their attitudes because they're operating according to a whole new dynamic, a whole new standard. They've been updrafted by the breeze of the Spirit. He's lifted them off the ground, so that they now can live at a level above.

WORST-CASE SCENARIO

Whatever the difficulties and the challenges you face now in life, you can be updrafted and picked up outside your natural self and lifted higher than you are now.

You may doubt that could ever be true in the current scenario of your circumstances. You may be saying, "There's just no hope. I just don't see how this situation will ever change." And in actuality, your situation might not change. It may even get worse. But your *relationship* to that situation can change, and it can change right now, immediately, and make all the difference in the world.

Maybe you're like the wife who keeps telling herself, "My husband's never going to change." (Ever felt that way about someone you know?) It's a thought that brings her nothing but grief and despair.

Let's take her word for it. And let's examine the worst-case scenario: Her husband will, in fact, never change, and she'll find it impossible on her own to deal with that changeless situation. That's the worst case. On the earthly level, it's an unendurable situation.

But if she's updrafted by the power of the Spirit, if she's lifted up and out of the limitations of that earthly perspective, then even though her husband never changes, she will have drastically changed the position from which she looks at him and at their relationship—and also at herself and at God. What was unendurable in that relationship becomes endurable. What was impossible becomes a means of experiencing God's presence and perspective on a deeper level than she ever thought possible. She has changed, even though there's no change in her situation.

Endurance with Joy

In whatever hardship or ordeal or difficulty you face, you may often feel like giving up. But if you quit before you've been updrafted, before you've waited in God's presence for all the power and strength His Spirit provides, before you've pursued the Holy One and His filling…then you've quit too soon. You've not gone all the way.

You see, the point of the Holy Spirit's power is not about shouting and jumping in a church service. The Holy Spirit's power is about enabling you to live on a supernatural level, with a supernatural experience of love and joy and peace and patience and kindness and goodness and faithfulness and gentleness and self-control—all those qualities that are so lacking in your natural self.

The Spirit's job is to cause you to live far above your ordinary capacity and inclination. His job is to get you to do stuff that, naturally speaking, you would never be inclined to do in serving God and others. His job is to cause you to act in supernatural love and holiness, and to respond to trials with a joy and a patience that you could never muster up on your own. When you're living that way—then you know you've found the real power of the Spirit.

In the book of Acts, the Holy Spirit transformed those first Christians from a band of folks hidden away behind closed doors to a bold force of men and women who "turned the world upside down" (17:6). What changed them? The blowing wind of the Holy Spirit's filling. It made the difference in their lives, and it did it from the inside out. They were all "filled with joy and with the Holy Spirit" (13:52).

That's the kind of joy that will keep you going without quitting. You may find some of your obligations and responsibilities in life to be unbearable. You may hate your job or your living situation. You may dislike some of your coworkers or your neighbors or your relatives or other people you have to deal with. But joy on your inside will keep you enduring...and only the Holy Spirit's updraft can bring you that joy in a lasting way.

The Spirit's job is to cause you to live far above your ordinary capacity and inclination. ■ ■ ■ ■ ■ ■ ■ ■ ■ ■ ■ ■

YOUr

ReSurreCtIOn

■ Are you ready for the Spirit to blow His fresh power and vitality in your direction? Are you ready to receive all that God wants to accomplish in your life in the way of restoration and renewal?

To help you prepare yourself for that breakthrough, I want to devote the rest of this book to asking you a few simple questions and discussing them with you. They'll help you examine this whole issue very personally and realistically and thoroughly, from several angles.

But before we dive into them, there's one thing I want to briefly clarify with you, something that represents the most thrilling aspect in Ezekiel's vision of the valley.

MORE THAN HISTORY

Remember again with me the climax of the promise Ezekiel heard: "Thus says the Lord GOD: Behold, I will open your graves and raise you from your graves, O my people" (Ezekiel 37:12)

That, for sure, is *resurrection.* If you were once dead and in your grave but now you've been raised up out of there, then you've definitely been resurrected. No doubt about it.

So with resurrection in mind, let's turn our attention in one particular direction—toward Jesus Christ. And specifically to something Jesus said on the occasion when He showed up late at the house of Mary and Martha in the village of Bethany. He was late, or so everyone supposed, because He'd been requested to come earlier when Lazarus, the brother of Mary and Martha, fell sick. By the time Jesus finally appeared, Lazarus had been dead four days.

Martha quickly conveyed her view that His delay was the only reason Lazarus was now dead instead of alive. When Jesus said, "Your brother will rise again," Martha naturally thought only of the distant eternal future—"I know that he will rise again in the resurrection on the last day" (John 11:23–24).

What Jesus spoke next were these amazing words: "I am the resurrection and the life" (v. 25).

He was talking about us, and He was talking about now.

∎ ∎ ∎ ∎ ∎ ∎ ∎ ∎ ∎ ∎ ∎

Please don't miss the significance of those words. He was not simply saying, "I Myself will personally rise from the dead." Nor was He saying, "I will bring resurrection life to people in the eternal future." He was saying much more. He was talking about *us,* and He was talking about *now.* And He went on to prove it.

At Eastertime, people all over the world celebrate the resurrection of Jesus Christ. Two thousand years ago, Jesus stepped forth from a tomb on a certain Sunday morning after His dead and crucified body had been placed there the previous Friday. His victory over death is a verifiable fact, the most important event in human history, and the guarantee of our own resurrection into eternity for all who believe.

But on that day in Bethany when Jesus declared, "I am the resurrection," He was saying, "Don't consign Me to history. Don't relegate Me to your annual remembrance or to your once-a-year church attendance. *I am* the resurrection. *I am* the definition of rising up from the dead. And right now, *I Myself* can raise to life anything that's dead in your existence."

WORTH WAITING FOR

Why did Jesus delay His coming to Bethany when Lazarus was sick? Because He wanted to let His followers see—empirically, experientially, visually—what it means that He actually *is* the resurrection.

Your personal circumstances may include dimensions and aspects that seem lifeless and hopeless. You have dreams or plans or relationships or abilities that seem to have died. It's been so bad for so long that it feels like rigor mortis has set in.

But in the midst of that numbness and powerlessness and helplessness, Jesus wants you to know the real truth. Not, "I *was* the resurrection," or even, "I *will be* the resurrection when your time on earth is over," but this: "I *am* the resurrection, right now, in your present situation." His resurrection has everything to do with anything that seems lifeless in your current experience.

He wants to do this for you because of His love for you. Just because Jesus was delayed in coming to Bethany doesn't mean He was lacking in care and concern for His good friend Lazarus or for Mary and Martha. In fact, when He arrived in Bethany that day, we read this about Him: "Jesus wept" (11:35). It's the shortest verse in the Bible, and there's a whole world of meaning in it. Here was a human situation where death had occurred, and the response which this brought forth from the heart of the Lord Jesus was weeping.

Be assured that even though the Lord may seem to be delayed in responding to your situation of loss and lifelessness and despair, He's still feeling what you're going through.

GIFT OF LIFE

Since Jesus Himself *is* the resurrection, what exactly does that mean for you and me?

It means especially that we who believe in our risen Savior and Lord can receive three gifts from Him. And He uses the story of Lazarus to illustrate each one for us, making a contemporary application to our generation and to every generation.

The first gift is the most obvious and dramatic—the gift of life. When Jesus approached the tomb of Lazarus, a cave with a stone over the opening, He gave this simple but astonishing command: "Take away the stone" (11:39).

At once, Martha asserted her practical nature. "Lord," she said, "by this time there will be an odor, for he has been dead four days" (v. 39). The weather was warm, and the corpse of her dead brother had been lying in that cave plenty long enough to cause unpleasant effects. "Let's get real," Martha was saying. "That man's flesh is rotting. Maggots have set in. If that rock is rolled away, we'll get hit by a stench that's like nothing we've ever experienced before!"

Have you ever had something die in your life, and the effect was so awful that your whole world seemed to smell rotten? It's like what happens when a chipmunk or a rat or some other varmint gets caught in your attic or your basement or the heating ducts in the walls and dies there. The resulting reek soon starts to permeate the whole house.

When Jesus asked for the tomb to be opened, Martha saw the situation heading from bad to worse. But Jesus answered her this way: "Did I not tell you that if you believed you would see the glory of God?" (v. 40). He was telling her, "Keep on believing, and you're going to see God show up and show off!" That's what glory is. And Martha and Mary and the village of Bethany were all about to see it.

Shock of a Lifetime

Jesus then turned to the tomb and gave a shout: "Lazarus, come out" (11:43). You were sick, Lazarus, and you died, you've been locked up lifeless and motionless and breathless in a tomb for four days, and furthermore, you stink. But now…get up and walk out of there *alive!*

That's all it took to make it happen. "The man who had died came out" (v. 44). The word of Jesus, the Messiah, the Son of God, had the authority to bring him out—because He Himself is the resurrection.

It's probably a good thing at this point that Jesus specifically called out the name of Lazarus. If He'd said only the words "Come out," all the other dead folks in that cemetery would have emerged from their tombs as well, which might have been more shock than the citizens of Bethany could handle in a day.

One resurrection was enough that day to make the point for all of us, for all time: Jesus can visit you in your deadly and smelly situa-tion, and out of it He can bring forth life, simply by calling your name.

He's the imparter of life wherever life is missing.

■ ■ ■ ■ ■ ■ ■ ■ ■ ■ ■

That's the good news of the gift of life in Jesus Christ. He wants you to know that He does more than just raise people from the dead; He raises them from dead situations. He's the imparter of life wherever life is missing.

Jesus stands outside the tomb of our lifeless situation and says, "Did I not tell you that if you believed you would see the glory of God?" Right now, He *Himself* is that which can show you the glory of God, no matter how difficult your circumstances.

Maybe He has delayed His coming to you, and in the mean-time, your situation has grown sicker and sicker, deader and deader, stinkier and stinkier. Why doesn't He show up? Because He's waiting for your faith to grow. He's waiting for you to believe. He assured us that if we believe, we would see God's glory; so it's only our slowness to believe that keeps us stuck in a grave.

Jesus says, *"I am* your resurrection; *I am* the answer to your death. Whatever is killing you, I am the cure, right now."

So why stay dead, when Jesus says, "Remove the stone"? Why hang around in a graveyard, when Jesus says, "Come out"? Why cling to the rottenness and the stench, when Jesus offers the gift of fresh new life? Nothing or nobody can make you feel as alive as Jesus Christ can.

NEVER FEAR

When Jesus told Martha, "I am the resurrection and the life," He immediately added these words: "Whoever believes in me, though he die, yet shall he live, and everyone who lives and believes in me shall never die" (11:25–26).

As believers in Christ, when do we die? *Never.* You have the promise of Jesus Himself on it.

The thing that represents humanity's greatest fear, the thing that people dread most, is the one thing that's sure to never happen to believers in Christ. Some people refuse to write out a will or to take out a life insurance policy because it would make them have to think about their death. Woody Allen once said, "I'm not afraid to die; I just don't want to be there when it happens."

Death carries a stigma, no matter what term you give it to try and soften the blow—"laid to rest," "passed away," "departed," "deceased." The central fact of our natural human condition cannot be softened. It's a fact. When a baby's born, that child has already begun the march to death. When a man brings his wife flowers, just give it time and the petals start falling off one by one— they're fast on their way to death, reminding us that we're the same way.

But the beautiful fact about knowing Jesus Christ is that you'll never die. Why? Because of the promise of Him who said, *"I am* the resurrection."* To be absent from the body is to be present with the Lord Jesus. Through our faith in Him, the moment we enter the experience that human beings call "death," we'll be immediately translated into the Lord's presence without ever experiencing the thing humanity fears most. Jesus has invaded that realm of death with His own resurrection from the dead, and in our experience, it means He's caused death itself to die.

Regardless of how old and rundown your physical existence becomes in this world, you're in possession of eternal life and all that it means. A hundred-dollar bill can get crumpled and faded and tattered and dirty, but it's still worth a hundred dollars. It hasn't lost its inherent value, and you can even trade it in at the bank for a brand new hundred-dollar bill. Because you belong to Jesus, you have inherent eternal value, a value that death can never touch or tarnish, no matter how dilapidated and worn and wrinkled your physical body becomes. And the day is approaching when you'll trade in that physical body for a new one that will last forever.

The beautiful fact about knowing Jesus Christ is that you'll never die.

■ ■ ■ ■ ■ ■ ■ ■ ■ ■ ■ ■

GIFT OF LIBERTY

At the command of Christ, Lazarus stepped forth from the tomb, "his hands and feet bound with linen strips, and his face wrapped with a cloth" (11:44). He was alive, but he still had his grave clothes on. He was still stuck in the trappings of death and needed to be set free.

So Jesus at once gave another command: "Unbind him, and let him go" (v. 44). He'd already given life to Lazarus; now He added the gift of liberty.

Jesus can unwrap you from whatever has been holding you hostage. He can loosen you from the things that have entangled you and tied you up. You've made wrong decisions and wrong turns, you've headed in wrong directions, and the result has been your captivity. You're tired of being bound and gagged and held hostage. You're tired of everything else controlling you instead of God controlling you.

The good news in Jesus Christ is that today is the day of your liberation. He's come to release you. He's come to set you free to become all that God made you to be, just like butterflies are freed when they leave the trappings of a cocoon and spread their new wings to fly.

So many people are needlessly unhappy because they've never soared upward to become what God created them to be. They're still trapped in caterpillar clothes. They're still cocooned in the old way. But Jesus sets you free to be what He made you to be. He was sent "to proclaim liberty to the captives" and "to set at liberty those who are oppressed" (Luke 4:18). And His freedom is true freedom: "If the Son sets you free, you will be free indeed" (John 8:36).

You don't have to spend any more time trying to be what other people tell you to be. You don't have to be the least concerned with the image that television or Hollywood holds up to you as the ideal. There's never any freedom in following that path. Jesus alone can set you on your personal road to perfect liberty. He alone can set you free for the purpose for which you've been created.

This liberty doesn't mean doing whatever you want. Instead it means being free to do whatever God wants; it means freedom to be all that He wants you to be.

He still has boundaries for us. After all, you can't have football freedom without sidelines. You can't have baseball freedom without foul lines. You can't have tennis freedom without baselines. You've got to have boundaries in order to express freedom. And within the perfect boundaries God provides, He sets us loose to attain and achieve our perfect fulfillment.

GIFT OF LOVE

There's a third precious gift that comes with the resurrection.

After raising Lazarus from the dead, Jesus soon visited Bethany again. "So they gave a dinner for him there. Martha served, and Lazarus was one of those reclining with him at the table" (John 12:2).

Jesus had given life and liberty to Lazarus, and now He added to them the opportunity for Lazarus to be *with* Him—to recline and dine with Him in intimate fellowship.

In His gift of resurrection, Jesus offers love as well as life and liberty. He wants to give you love so you don't have to keep searching for it in all the wrong places. You've looked high and low, and you've tried to settle for a little satisfaction here and a little fulfillment there, yet none of it works for long. But Jesus says, "I'm what you're looking for forever, because *I am* the resurrection."

He puts it this way in the book of Revelation: "Behold, I stand at the door and knock. If anyone hears my voice and opens the door, I will come in to him and eat with him, and he with me" (3:20).

Intimacy breeds life.

■ ■ ■ ■ ■ ■ ■ ■ ■ ■ ■ ■

In the Bible, eating isn't mostly about food. Eating in the Bible is mostly about fellowship. God doesn't want any impersonal distance in your relationship with Him; He wants closeness. He wants it to be like having a candlelight dinner together. He's offering you intimacy of relationship, because intimacy breeds life.

A woman who's pregnant didn't get that way by looking in a mirror. She got that way because intimacy occurred, and intimacy has a way of breeding new life. And others will always find out when a woman is carrying this new life, because it has a way of becoming visible. She can hide it for a little while, but as that new life begins to pulsate within her and grow, it will manifest itself, and she won't be able to keep it to herself any longer.

That's also how others know when we're experiencing intimacy with Jesus. As we recline with Jesus, we get pregnant with the reality of God's glory inside us, and then it grows and it shows. There's a gleam in our eye and a liveliness in our step. There's a joy and peace in our attitude. And there's love and patience in our relationships. It's an expression of new life…all because of the presence of the One who says, "*I am* the resurrection."

Is it showing in your life?

If not—then know for sure that Jesus is still in a resurrection mood today. He's still summoning forth the dead from their tombs. God is still calling out His promise from the valley of dry bones: "Behold, I will open your graves and raise you from your graves" (Ezekiel 37:12).

Onward

And now it's time to proceed with those simple questions I mentioned earlier, to take us through the rest of this book.

I trust that you'll reflect seriously on them and answer them honestly and that they'll help you discover God's sufficient supply for all your spiritual needs...so you can step forth anew from life-lessness and dryness and enjoy a resurrection life of consistent passion and celebration.

PART II

Deepening Your spiritual passion

are You Hungry?

■ One day when I was speaking at a chapel meeting for one of the NFL teams, a player came up afterward and told me, "I can't seem to find time to have devotions."

I told him his definition of the problem was incorrect. He had a hunger problem, not a time management problem. Because when you're hungry, you don't have to find time to eat. When your stomach is growling, it shows up in your choices. Hungry people don't wait for food to happen upon them. They make their way to it. They change the direction they're driving in order to stop where food is. When you're truly hungry, you adjust your life to make time for a meal.

Another member of that football team came up to me and said, "I've prayed to God about a stronghold in my life, but it hasn't gone away. I'm praying sincerely. So what am I doing wrong?"

I responded, "If you're praying about a stronghold in your life that won't go away, then God is telling you He wants you to go deeper." When we can't find release from a burden that we've been sincerely praying about it, if we're not yet victorious, then we know God wants us to go deeper in intimacy with Him. We're not yet as close to Him as He wants us to be. There's still too much distance, and we've got to close the gap. We've let ourselves feel satisfied when God wants us to feel hungrier.

The Bible declares over and over and over again that God feeds hungry people. But only hungry people. One of the greatest promises in the Bible is this one that Jesus makes: "Blessed are those who hunger and thirst for righteousness, for they shall be satisfied" (Matthew 5:6).

CHECK YOUR APPETITE

As we begin the last part of this book, my first question for you is this: Are you hungry for the spiritual renewal that God promises? *Desperately* hungry?

When athletes want to get to the next level or move from the bench to a starting position, the coach will often ask them, "How hungry are you? How bad do you want it?" That's what God wants to know from us as well.

One way doctors determine the health of an individual is related to appetite. The loss of a desire for food is an indication that something deeper is wrong. When you lose your appetite, something inside isn't working properly, because hunger is a natural part of a proper functioning life.

Hunger is the prerequisite for spiritual passion.

■ ■ ■ ■ ■ ■ ■ ■ ■ ■ ■ ■

How, then, do we explain Christians who have no spiritual appetite, who don't have hunger for God? It indicates a spiritual problem.

Hunger is the prerequisite for spiritual passion, and the Bible shows us many helpful pictures of how that hunger manifests itself. Let's take a look at one of them.

THE UP-AND-OUTER

Zacchaeus was someone you could call an up-and-outer. He had a plush job, working in Jericho for the Roman Empire's equivalent of the IRS, heading up a regional office. "He was a chief tax collector and was rich," Luke tells us (19:2).

But in Israel in those days, tax collectors were among the most despised people around. They were viewed as Benedict Arnolds because they were Jewish men working for the Roman government to exact taxes from fellow Jews at exorbitant rates. They not only got a salary from Rome for their work, but they would also cushion the taxes for their own economic benefit. If Rome wanted 25 percent, the tax collector might charge 35 percent and keep the extra 10 percent in addition to his salary. They were crooks, and people viewed them as the lowest of the low.

And Zacchaeus was one of them, though he was economically sufficient and needed nothing from anyone, because he'd become wealthy. His prosperity came at the expense of popularity.

He might easily have shrugged off his bad reputation and simply been content with his position and his resources, but Luke tells us that this man "was seeking to see who Jesus was" (v. 3) on the day the Savior came through Jericho. Word had gotten out about this Galilean, this miracle worker from Nazareth. Zacchaeus just had to see Him.

But it wasn't working out. Luke says that Zacchaeus tried to see Jesus, "but on account of the crowd he could not, because he was small of stature" (v. 3). Zacchaeus was a short guy, and every time he tried to catch a glimpse of Jesus, other people got in the way. The masses blocked his view.

FINDING A WAY

At this point, he could have simply given up and said, "Well, maybe another time, another place; it's just too crowded here today." He might have walked away complaining, "If only I wasn't so short. If only I didn't have this heredity problem where my view is always blocked by everybody else."

But Zacchaeus didn't do any of that. He wasn't about to let circumstances or other people stop him from realizing his desperate desire to see Jesus. "So he ran on ahead and climbed up into a sycamore tree to see him, for he was about to pass that way" (19:4). Zacchaeus decided he was going to make this thing happen.

The other day I was talking with a young single lady who was trying to find out whether a certain gentleman was serious about her. She hoped his interest was there, but she wasn't sure, and she was trying to weigh things by discussing their relationship with me. In the course of our conversation, I asked her, "How often does he call you?"

"Oh, once a week," she answered. "Or sometimes every two weeks."

So I responded, "I don't know whether or not this man's going to get there...but trust me, he's not there yet." When a man's interest in someone is really there, he'll find a way to connect with her as often as possible, or at least more than once every week or two.

Zacchaeus was there. He was dead serious. He was so hungry to see Jesus that he set aside his dignity to do it. You see, a chief tax collector—or a chief anything—doesn't go around climbing trees. If you're the chief, you just don't do that because it makes you look like a fool. You do it only if what you want to see from that treetop is bigger than who you think you are and if your hunger and your desperation drives you to do it.

When you get desperate, you take desperate measures.

Our problem so often today is that we aren't really hungry yet. We aren't desperate. Because when you get desperate, you take desperate measures and don't care who's watching. Zacchaeus didn't care that a crowd watched him climb that tree. He didn't care if they observed him up a tree and out on a limb because he was desperate to get his hunger satisfied.

Starving Inside

What made Zacchaeus different from the rest of the crowd that day? We could probably describe that crowd as the Jesus Fan Club. Jesus had been going around performing miracles, and who doesn't want to see a miracle? He'd been going around bestowing blessings, and who doesn't want a blessing? Everybody wanted to hang on Jesus' cloak because, after all, He was putting on the best show in town—healing the sick, raising the dead, casting out demons.

But Zacchaeus had something deeper going on. He was hungry on the inside. He was hungry for forgiveness. He was starving because of his sin, and he wasn't going to let anybody or any amount of people stop him from seeing Jesus that day.

When a baby has been sleeping in his mother's arms and his hunger stirs him awake, he doesn't care if it's eleven o'clock Sunday morning and his mother happens to be sitting in a church service listening to the pastor preach. That baby will burst out crying because he cares about only one thing: Who's going to feed me?

Zacchaeus gave up his dignity to get a look at Jesus because he was hungry for what Jesus could feed him. And Jesus responded.

You know what happened next. Jesus looked up in that tree, called Zacchaeus by name, and invited Himself to this man's house. So Zacchaeus "hurried and came down and received him joyfully" (19:6). And in the next few hours, right in his own home with Jesus as his guest, this crooked tax collector learned that what Jesus had to offer was exactly what he'd hoped for and so desperately needed: "And Jesus said to him, 'Today salvation has come to this house, since he also is a son of Abraham. For the Son of Man came to seek and to save the lost'" (vv. 9–10).

DETACHED FROM THE CROWD

On the streets of Jericho that day, why did the name of
Zacchaeus get called out by the voice of God's Son? Why this
man and not others? Because Zacchaeus was a hungry sinner.
Trust me, that crowd was full of sinners, and most of them were
hungry too—but not in the right way. They were hungry for what
they could see Jesus *do;* they weren't hungry for Jesus. They were
hungry for His blessings, but they weren't in hot pursuit of
Jesus Himself. Zacchaeus, on the other hand, climbed the tree
of destiny, and as a result, God's salvation was poured out on a
desperate man.

We know Zacchaeus was different from all the rest of that
crowd, because when the others saw Jesus go inside this man's
house, "they all grumbled, 'He has gone in to be the guest of a man
who is a sinner'" (19:7). This just didn't fit their theology. It didn't
match their understanding. It didn't make sense, which tells us
they really didn't know who Jesus was.

How many of them grumbled? "All." So they each had something in common with one another, something that none of them
had in common with Zacchaeus.

Zacchaeus wasn't just part of the crowd. Remember how he
"ran on ahead" of them to climb the tree? He broke off from them
because something was essentially true about him that wasn't essentially true about all the others there that day.

What was their problem? They'd become so enamored with
the miracles of Jesus that they lost sight of the mission of Jesus,
the mission He articulated right there in a tax collector's living
room: "For the Son of Man came to seek and to save the lost"
(v. 10).

The Son of Man majors in sinners. He doesn't major in sin—he majors in sinners. But then, everybody's a sinner, so what kind of sinner does He focus on?

Hungry ones. Desperate ones. And still today, Jesus gives His attention to sinners who desperately want Him to address their sin because of who they know He is.

Could it be that many of us are just too righteous for Jesus? We're too "okay" for Jesus. We're part of the crowd. We haven't yet broken loose to go climb the sycamore. We haven't discovered that unless you're galvanized into Jesus' mission, you'll miss Jesus.

Jesus is about separating sinners from their sin. He's not about doing miraculous tricks for folks. The miracles He did in the New Testament were real, they were authentic, and they were verifiable, but they were for a purpose. Jesus didn't do miracles to flex His muscles; He did miracles to emphasize His mission.

The Son of Man majors in sinners.

RESCUE MISSION

If you're genuinely hungry, then let me assure you that in your own life there's a sycamore tree nearby for you to climb. And you can position yourself there to experience Jesus' mission, just as Zacchaeus did.

God's got something He wants to give away to the hungry man or woman or boy or girl who doesn't just want to be part of the crowd. He has something for those who know their spiritual need, and are desperate enough that they're not concerned about a loss of dignity in climbing a sycamore tree.

When paramedics rush to the aid of someone who's hurting, they move back the bystanders who are just there watching. They clear them away because paramedics have one goal in mind: to assist and rescue the hurting. Jesus has one goal in mind: to get to sinners who've become hungry for forgiveness and salvation and deliverance. He hasn't come for righteous folk who don't need repentance. Nor has He come to hear people justify their sin. He came to separate sinners from their sin. He came to see the same kind of genuine, radical repentance that Zacchaeus demonstrated: "Behold, Lord, the half of my goods I give to the poor. And if I have defrauded anyone of anything, I restore it fourfold" (19:8).

Don't fail to notice that Zacchaeus called Jesus "Lord." Something changed in Zacchaeus. This traitor, this turncoat, had a radical transformation. He still had a ways to go; he didn't become a perfect man. But in the presence of his Lord, something changed. If we want Jesus to be only our Savior and not our Lord, we won't experience the life-change; we won't receive His gift of renewal. If there's no Lord, there's no change. Or let me put it this way. The sooner you say "Lord," the sooner you'll see change.

Are you hungry to see that transformation? Are you in desperate need of what only the Lord can give? Are you willing to do something more than just be in the vicinity of the Lord along with the crowd? Are you desperate enough to stop letting people get in the way? Desperate enough to climb that sycamore tree?

If you are, be encouraged, because that very hunger is the prerequisite for spiritual passion.

Emptiness and Filling

Exactly how hungry are you? Is it a gnawing sense of emptiness that desperately needs to be filled?

Never lose sight of this principle: The amount of your emptiness will determine the amount of your filling. You'll never discover that God is all you need until He's all you have. Do you sense your true need for God? Or is your life too crowded for that?

To make room for the new thing God wants to do inside of you, old things must go. It's hard for God to bring about something new within us if we're still crowded inside with old stuff. When we aren't seeing more of God's power, more of God's breakthroughs, more of God's presence, more of God's dynamite, it's simply because we're too full of something else for God to fill us.

So here's the question again: How hungry are you? Now, I know you want a spiritual breakthrough. I know you want power and victory in your life. But that's not my question. My question is: How hungry are you...for God? Are you hungry enough to look to Him alone as your first and last resort? Or are you still trying to do things on your own without Him? If so, you're not hungry enough yet. You're not starving.

God is looking for growling stomachs. He's looking for people whose spiritual insides are rumbling for Him.

We're too full of something else for God to fill us.

■ ■ ■ ■ ■ ■ ■ ■ ■ ■ ■ ■

Junk Food and Diet Pills

The reason many of us aren't hungry inside like we should be is that we're full of the wrong stuff. We've satisfied ourselves with snacks and have left no room for the true stuff that's needed for our spiritual nutritional development.

Are you hungry for the true spiritual food? Or are you trying to satisfy your hunger with junk food?

If you eat enough snacks, it becomes a cheap substitute for addressing legitimate hunger, and you lose your appetite for the real thing. Too many of us are still snacking on God. We want a sermon snack here, a song snack there, and a bite-sized one-minute morning devotional now and then. All we're doing is nibbling at the table. There's no passionate pursuit of God. And God will never bless your snacks.

God doesn't want you content with spiritual fast-food or drive-through food, something you can just pick up and gulp down while you continue your other business. And He doesn't want Christian nibblers and Christian samplers. He wants you to come and dine at His table. He wants those who will take time to enter into His presence, who won't be satisfied with just hearing a weekly sermon, because the best sermon in the world is only a snack if it doesn't make you passionately pursue God the rest of the week.

People who want to lose weight often try diet pills. The pills don't remove hunger; they only suppress it. You're still hungry. You just don't know you're hungry because the pills' effect has concealed the inner reality. Many of us don't feel spiritually hungry because we've taken things into our minds and hearts that act as spiritual hunger-suppressants, so we don't feel as hungry as we ought to feel. We don't feel as needy of spiritual food as we really are.

It's like we've become satisfied with only a pacifier in our mouth. But you can be sucking on a pacifier and still be starving to death.

Increasing Your Capacity

I recall a time when I and a group of others in our church were fasting for a week in conjunction with a time of "solemn assembly" to begin the new year. Needless to say, I was greatly anticipating my first meal after the fast. We went to someone's home for it, and I remember well the enticing sight and aroma of pancakes and eggs and bacon and lots more.

But to my great discouragement and dismay, after taking just a few bites, I felt stuffed. The others who had been fasting that week shared the same sensation. We couldn't eat very much, and of course the reason was that our extended time without food had greatly diminished our capacity. Our stomachs had shrunk.

Many of us spend much of our week fasting from God, and when we come to church on Sunday, it seems to be plenty to satisfy our spiritual appetite. Our capacity is restricted. But if you want to get more of God, that capacity has to be expanded.

The reason some Christians are able to feast on God while others only nibble is that they have differing capacities. Those who are in hot pursuit of the Holy keep expanding their capacity, and they want to eat all the time. They want as much of God as they can possibly get. But God will give us only as much of Him as we can possibly handle. He'll never give us more of Himself than our spiritual system is able to inculcate.

True spiritual power and passion require spiritual capacity.

And spiritual capacity comes only through spiritual intimacy. And spiritual intimacy comes only from spiritual hunger. Or let me put it another way: The hungrier for God you are, the more intimate you are with Him. The more intimate you are, the more capacity you have. And the more capacity you have, the more power and passion you experience.

True spiritual passion requires spiritual capacity.

⬛ ⬛ ⬛ ⬛ ⬛ ⬛ ⬛ ⬛ ⬛ ⬛ ⬛ ⬛

LET HIM KNOW

If you know you're hungry for God, tell Him: "Lord, I'm hungry for You." If you *want* to be hungry for God, but you've been snacking so much that you aren't sure whether you really are or not, then ask Him to create and reveal that true hunger in you. If you want a greater capacity for Him so you can experience more of His presence and power and supernatural intervention, then determine to bring that desire before Him as an urgent request.

And that brings us to the next question I want to talk with you about.

are You asking?

■ God wants people who are passionately pursuing Him, who throw themselves upon Him with a desperation that cries out. Whenever you come across people in the Bible who are crying out, what you're hearing is desperation. Someone who cries out is someone who's dead serious.

Let me repeat what I said earlier: You'll never discover that God is all you need until He's all you have. And when your awareness of your need gets that strong and that desperate, you're not sophisticated anymore; you don't pray cute prayers or rote prayers anymore. You cry out. You plead.

FRIENDSHIP WITH GOD

Moses was someone who cried out for God. Here was a man who was called God's friend—"The Lord used to speak to Moses face to face, as a man speaks to his friend" (Exodus 33:11). They got personal. There was total openness and candor in their relationship.

No pretense. No formulas. No agendas. No holding back. Just simple honesty and sharing.

It's the relational truth that's reflected in something Jesus told His disciples: "I have called you friends, for all that I have heard from my Father I have made known to you" (John 15:15). To be God's friend is to enjoy the intimacy of His continuous presence. He isn't satisfied with a casual relationship or with occasional encounters. He wants an intimate, close-up friendship.

What brought about that friendship for Moses? It was God's gracious response to fill the passionate hunger Moses had for Him. It was His *favor* poured out on Moses, and Moses knew it.

Communication was at the heart of this friendship. Moses would go and talk with God (in the "tent of meeting" [Exodus 33:7–9]), and God would talk to Moses. It was two-way dialogue.

The ability to communicate is always at the heart of a meaningful friendship, at the heart of relational intimacy. When communication is strong, relationships are strong. When communication breaks down, relationships break down.

The ability to communicate is always at the heart of relational intimacy.

■ ■ ■ ■ ■ ■ ■ ■ ■ ■ ■ ■

A BIGGER VIEW OF PRAYER

You already know that communication with God is called prayer. It's something we're commanded to do "without ceasing" (1 Thessalonians 5:17). We're to talk with God all the time. Which means we can't look at the full picture of prayer as a separate, formalized activity—as a ritual to perform or a program to complete.

Prayer means bringing God to bear on everything, with no area of life excluded. There's nothing in our experience that we aren't to interact with Him about—no problem, circumstance, need, opportunity, struggle, victory, frustration, pleasure, or irritation where He isn't brought into our consciousness of what we're going through.

By its very nature then, unceasing prayer will not be an isolated activity. If we're faithful to obey this command, then most of the time we spend in prayer won't be on our knees. We still need to have set-aside times for concentrated prayer without distraction. But even if we spend a couple of hours at it each day, that represents only a small fraction of our time, though an extremely important fraction. There's a balance of at least twenty-two hours of our day that are *not* spent on our knees, and yet even in those moments we're to be praying.

So how do you do it?

It's simple. You consciously bring God to bear on everything. And you do that not through long, drawn-out prayers, but through sentence prayers. You whisper them, either with your lips or in your mind. "Lord, I need Your wisdom now to be able to handle this conversation." "Lord, I'm facing this struggle and I don't know how to deal with it apart from You, so I'm leaning on You." Each time you do that, you're praying. You're concentrating Godward. And as you develop this habit of intimacy, of talking to God about everything all day long, you can't help but get closer to Him.

So don't get locked into thinking that your prayers at breakfast this morning have satisfied your need for intimacy with God. They haven't. God wants to be part of every aspect of your life. And that means you should pray without ceasing. He wants to be involved. He wants you to talk to Him about everything. That's what real friends do. And it's what Moses did with God.

THE REASON FOR MEDITATION

And God responded back to Moses. He "used to speak to Moses face to face" (Exodus 33:11) in the tent of meeting. But we don't have that same arrangement. How will God talk with you and me? How do we make ourselves available to actually hear His voice?

There's a word for it in the Bible. It's *meditation.* Meditation is focusing undivided attention on God, through His Word, the Bible. It means emptying your mind of all distractions and focusing all your inner attention on God through His Word. And please don't misread what was just stated. I didn't say focus on the Word of God, but focus on God *through* His Word. When you focus on the Bible without focusing on God, the Bible then becomes an informational textbook, and that approach can be deadly to your spiritual health. You could actually be ruining your spiritual life in your Bible study. Just ask a seminary student who studies the Scriptures academically, just to get a grade—after four years of that in seminary, he has a lot more information about the Bible, but he may just end up worse off spiritually.

God didn't give us the Bible merely to provide us with more academic information about Him, or even more inspiration about Him. He gave us the Bible to offer us more *revelation* of Himself. And revelation means God Himself disclosing Himself.

God still speaks today.

▪ ▪ ▪ ▪ ▪ ▪ ▪ ▪ ▪ ▪ ▪ ▪

Anyone who is passionately pursuing intimacy, walking with God and including Him in everything, will get to hear God's voice. God still speaks today. He always speaks through His Word. He always speaks in a manner consistent with His Word, never in contradiction to His Word, but He applies His Word personally and specifically to individuals. If you're close friends with God—if you're pursuing intimacy with Him—then He takes His truth in the Scriptures and applies it to your unique situation. You'll hear Him for yourself. When God tells you, you're going to *know*. And there's nothing more potent than knowing what *God* says to *you*.

FAVOR WITH GOD

In one of his prayers to God, Moses expressed why he felt free to make the requests that he was making. It was because the Lord Himself had told him, "I know you by name, and you have also found favor in my sight" (Exodus 33:12). It's hard to get God to tell you His secrets if you haven't found favor. Having His favor means that God is happy with you. He's content with you. He feels good about you. Moses could pray, "You're happy with our rela-tionship, so now You can show me deeper things. Now You can show me exactly what to do in this situation." Don't ask God to tell you His secrets if you don't have His favor through the intimacy of your relationship with Him.

Maybe you're facing a crisis now and you need God to show you His intentions. But that's something He'll do only if you've found favor with Him.

Have you ever phoned a beautician or barber because something came up—an emergency, an unexpected occasion where you needed to look your best—and you needed them to fit you in? Let me tell you how to make sure they fit you in. Just be a faithful, regular, paying customer *before* your emergency. If you still owe them for your last visit, they may not fit you in. If you use their services only occasionally, they may decide you can just go to your other beautician or barber and let them fit you in. But if the right relationship is there, if you've found favor with them beforehand, then they'll be glad to help you out.

Many of us, when we face a sudden crisis, will go to God and ask Him to fit us in, but we haven't been faithful and regular in coming to Him beforehand.

But Moses had been faithful and regular. So he came before God and said, "If I have found favor in your sight, please show me now your ways, that I may know you in order to find favor in your sight" (Exodus 33:13). He wanted to know God's *ways*—His habits and behavior, His intentions and plans, His attitudes and approaches. Moses knew that the better He knew God's ways, the better He knew God.

Have you ever prayed like that? "God, show me Your ways! I want to know You."

AT A CRITICAL TIME

This particular prayer from Moses happened at a very critical time for him. It was a crisis moment, and he desperately needed direction. The people of Israel had just built an idol—a golden calf—after God gave Moses His Law. Now God was angry with them. Moses was supposed to lead these people into the Promised Land, but now things were stalled. There was some confusion and uncertainty and inertia. Moses knew he needed to learn more of the ways of God in order to better understand the path he was to take and his own responsibilities. Things were dim and fuzzy right now, and Moses needed God to turn on a light switch.

Moses was saying, "God, I have some unclarity about my next move. Things are not fully clear to me. I know You brought me to this point, but the next leg of our journey is uncertain to me. So let me in on what *You* are thinking. Let me know *Your* ways. Let me know what *You* have planned. Clarify *Your* intentions for me. Because only then can I better know You, and only by better knowing You can I really know what I need to do. I need discernment before I can go forward, before I can recognize the proper path before me. And I know I'll get it only if You reveal it to me. You're going to have to show me."

God is free to share His secrets with you as you ask for them.

■ ■ ■ ■ ■ ■ ■ ■ ■ ■ ■ ■ ■

Moses wasn't asking for mere information; he was asking for *illumination.* Information is data that's tied to raw facts, and information is critical. But Moses wasn't asking God to write down a list of facts and data and instructions. Moses was saying, "Disclose *Yourself* to me." Moses needed clarity, and he knew that if he was going to get it, it would only be because God revealed it to him.

One of the great fruits of growing close to God is asking and receiving information that leads to illumination. God is free to share His secrets with you as you ask for them. And nothing is more valuable to you than that, especially in those times when the future direction in your life is fuzzy, or when you're in a crisis situation. We need God to turn the light on. We need to see, with fresh urgency, His divine purpose and direction for us. We want that clarity before we go forward. And it's all a matter of prayer.

FOR US, NOT JUST ME

The next thing Moses asked for was God's continuing presence among His people. Moses prayed for the people of Israel and pleaded for God to guide them.

This request came about because even though Moses had found favor with God, the people of Israel as a whole had not. In fact, God was ticked off with Israel. While Moses had been on the mountain meeting with God, the people had been worshiping idols. The first commandment had gone by the wayside.

So God told Moses, "My presence will go with *you,* and I will give *you* rest" (33:14)—and that "you" was singular. But Moses boldly asked God to extend that promise to the entire nation, and he mentioned why: "Is it not in your going with us, so that we are distinct, I and your people, from every other people on the face of the earth?" (33:16).

Moses was saying, "I'm glad to have You for me, Lord God, but this whole situation is bigger than me. So my prayer is not just for me. I need You to go with *us*. I'm nothing without You, and *we* are nothing without You—and I want us to know Your presence on the highest possible level."

It's the same situation when you get on your knees for your family or for your church or for others you love. You sense His wonderful love and purpose for yourself, but You want Him to extend it to others. "God, I have a wife and three children, and we need You to be with *us*." "God, there are five hundred of us in this church, and I ask You to be with *us*." And we'll know that His presence is with us when we're "distinct" from the world. We'll have a testimony that marks us off as different.

GOING FOR GLORY

Moses didn't stop there. He didn't ease up on his passionate praying. As he and God talked together, Moses added this request: "Please show me your glory" (33:18).

This is as deep as you can get. You can't get more profound than this, because God's glory is the sum total of His perfections. God's glory is God *seen;* it's the divine essence revealed. It's observing His personality at work.

God's glory is the actual manifestation of His attributes. It's one thing for us to say that God is omnipotent, that He's all powerful. It's quite another thing to *see* that power. It's one thing to say that God is everywhere, that He's omnipresent. It's another thing to see Him show up where you need Him right now. It's one thing to say that God is sovereign. And He is—He sits as the controller of the universe. But it's another thing to actually see Him take charge of your mess.

It's one thing to know God's attributes and be able to recite them; it's quite another to see them show up. And that's what Moses wants to see when he says, "Show me Your glory." He's saying, "Let me see Your perfection unveiled in front of my eyes."

Straight to the Core

Moses, of course, had already seen some wild stuff from the hand of God. He'd seen a bush that wouldn't burn and heard God's voice speaking from it. At God's command he saw his shepherd's crook turn into a snake and become a shepherd's crook again. He'd seen the devastating results of ten divine plagues upon Egypt. He'd seen the parting of the Red Sea, and he'd seen it sweep back over Pharaoh's army. He'd witnessed fire and thunder on Mount Sinai when God gave him the Ten Commandments.

We're not talking about a novice here who's now asking to see God's glory. So why, when a person has seen all of that, would he be asking God to show him His glory?

The more you see of Him, the more you know that there's so much more to see.

■ ■ ■ ■ ■ ■ ■ ■ ■ ■ ■ ■ ■

This man was after something. Moses had begun to see that there's always so much more to God. There's so much infinitude in God, so much limitlessness. The more you see of Him, the more you know that there's so much more to see. And Moses wanted to get to the radical core of it.

God Answers Moses

Moses didn't utter those words just to receive a personal blessing or just to satisfy intellectual curiosity. His purpose was to witness and experience the core of who God is, the essential reality of who He is. How do we know that?

Because of how his request was answered. God first responded, "I will make all my goodness pass before you and will proclaim before you my name 'The LORD.' And I will be gracious to whom I will be gracious, and will show mercy on whom I will show mercy" (33:19). So God was going to let Moses experience quite a lot—His "goodness" (His splendor or beauty), plus His grace and mercy, plus the proclamation of God's name, Yahweh, *I AM,* which means the self-existent, all-sufficient One. This was the culmination of God's attributes.

But then He added these words to Moses: "You cannot see my face, for man shall not see me and live" (v. 20).

Moses had grown in his intimate hunger for God to the point that he could boldly ask to see the very face of God. And the Lord had to tell him that this was impossible—no human being could see His full, exposed essence because it would kill that person instantly. God's glory is like a super-ultra radiation zone that pierces into everything that gets close and overpowers it. Our limited humanity, compared with God's infinite holiness, just doesn't allow for such a thing.

Physically speaking, it would be like our trying to take a visit to the sun. It would be a wasted trip. No need for anyone to expect us back to talk about our experiences and pass around photographs.

And yet, in a real sense, Moses' request to see God's glory was eventually answered—fifteen hundred years after he died. It was on the occasion when Jesus Christ, the incarnate Son of God, climbed a high mountain and was transfigured there, "and his face shone like the sun, and his clothes became white as light" (Matthew 17:2). Then Moses appeared there (with Elijah) and spoke with Jesus. And the experience was more than worth waiting for.

MORE AND MORE

Moses was allowed to see more of God than you or I have ever seen—but it was only a glimpse. There was still infinitely more to hunger for and ask for.

God will be faithful to satisfy your authentic hunger for Him as you bring it to Him in prayer. And then, in humble worship, you'll be able to pray as Job did, "I had heard of you by the hearing of the ear, but now my eye sees you" (Job 42:5).

As God lets you see more and more of Himself...will you keep going back to Him, hungering and asking for more?

are YOU Drawing Near?

■ Decades ago, before the era of mandatory seat belts for automobile passengers, you could always tell which couples were in love and which ones weren't. You knew things were going well in a relationship when you saw the wife or girlfriend snuggled up close beside her man at the steering wheel. And you knew things were cooling off when she sat close to the door. That distance indicated something was gone from their love relationship, especially when the distance became permanent.

Many of God's children are content to ride in the car with the Lord, but they want to keep their distance. But God wants us to have a desire for intimacy that keeps us sliding toward Him ever closer.

To put it another way, He isn't interested simply in a legal contract with you or me. He's not content for there to be a scroll in heaven that lists your name among the redeemed. The legal side of it is important—it's called being justified. When you place your faith in Christ alone for the forgiveness of sins and the gift of eternal life, your name is written in the Lamb's book of life and you're legally declared righteous. But God wants more than that.

Everyone who comes to Jesus Christ for salvation is legally married to Him. But we all know there's a big difference between legal marriage and an intimate relationship. God isn't satisfied that one day you came forward to the altar to solidify a marriage relationship with Him. He wants the intimacy that such a marriage is meant to bring about.

God also says that by virtue of your salvation in Christ, you're now His child, His son or daughter. Are you making the most of it by pursuing intimacy with your Father? God doesn't want visiting hours; He wants full custody.

> God doesn't want visiting hours; He wants full custody.
>
> ■ ■ ■ ■ ■ ■ ■ ■ ■ ■ ■ ■

HIS INVITATION

If you're desperately hungry for the Lord, and if you're taking that hunger to Him in prayer, you can expect to hear His clear invitation to draw near to Him—to come in closer.

So my next question for you in this book is this: Will you accept that invitation to move in His direction in order to experience greater intimacy with your Creator and your Savior and your Lord?

It's a question of positioning. It's a question of placement and direction in regard to the focus of your heart and your life. And the response is all up to you, because we can actually be in the vicinity of the Lord and yet hold back and not draw near.

Let me show you from the Bible what I mean.

ISSUES

In the fifth chapter of Mark's gospel we encounter one of the most striking portraits of desperation in the Scriptures.

Here's how Mark begins painting this picture for us: "And there was a woman who had had a discharge of blood for twelve years, and who had suffered much under many physicians, and had spent all that she had, and was no better but rather grew worse" (5:25–26).

This woman had what we could call a uterine hemorrhage, a constant bleeding that couldn't be stopped. The old King James Version calls it "an issue of blood," and in her case I like that word *issue.* We can say with certainty that this woman had issues, because she faced more than just a medical problem.

She also faced a financial issue. Of course in those days no one enjoyed the luxury of medical insurance, and this woman had totally depleted her financial sustenance to pay for treatment from a number of doctors. Yet for all their poking and prodding, these physicians only made her condition worse instead of better. They just didn't know how to solve this problem. And you know how easy it is to get ticked off when you pay somebody to fix something and it's still broken after paying them.

We can also see that this woman probably had a psychological problem, as evidenced by how she was sneaking around that day. "She had heard the reports about Jesus and came up behind him in the crowd" (v. 27). Now, it's no wonder the woman used this approach. Her medical problem was a rather embarrassing kind of illness. It wasn't a condition you would go around discussing openly, and in fact you would be forced to take pains to try and keep it from being noticed.

Reinforcing her embarrassment and her psychological damage was the fact that she had a spiritual and social issue. The book of Leviticus tells us that in the Jewish law, when a woman had a discharge of blood, she was considered ceremonially unclean (15:25–31). This required separation from the community, because everything she touched—or anyone who touched her—was considered unclean as well. Even after her discharge of blood had ended, the period of uncleanness continued for seven additional days. But in the case of this woman Mark tells us about, the flow of blood had probably never entirely stopped for that long—which meant her time of ceremonial cleanness never came. And all this had gone on for twelve years—socially she became an outcast. In fact, we aren't even given her name.

This woman's total life was one big issue. She was defiled, destitute, discouraged, and desperate. She must have felt as useless and hopeless as a pile of dry bones in that valley Ezekiel saw.

We all know what it's like to have a bad day, but we learn to endure and get beyond it. Lots of us can relate as well to what it means to carry on through a bad month or even a bad year. But to go year after year after year with the kind of problems this woman faced would probably be more than most of us could take.

WHAT DESPERATION WILL DO

There's something about getting desperate. There's something about being in a hopeless situation and in grave need of help—when you've tried everything you can think of and everything money could buy, yet you've still come up short and your life is in shambles—there's something about that situation that brings God's truth into focus as never before and makes it look better than ever.

In Mark 5, Jesus was in town, and word had gotten out about Him. Word had gotten out that He's good with issues. Word had gotten out of how He'd been helping so many people. And the truth dawned on this woman: "Jesus can help *me* with *my* issues." Here was her last and only hope.

Yet there was a problem: With growing conviction she recognized what He could do for her, but this woman wasn't in Jesus' appointment book. In fact, at the moment when she caught sight of Him and wanted His attention, Jesus' time was already being taken by someone else—someone who was needy like her, but who unlike her was prominent and had a position in society and a recognized identity—"one of the rulers of the synagogue, Jairus by name" (v. 22).

Before telling us about the woman with the hemorrhage, Mark tells us how this important man approached Jesus and "fell at his feet and implored him earnestly, saying, 'My little daughter is at the point of death. Come and lay your hands on her, so that she may be made well and live'" (vv. 22–23). So Jesus went with Jairus at once to heal this little girl. "And a great crowd followed him and thronged about him" (v. 24).

In the midst of the surging throng was this bleeding, desperate woman. Here was someone penniless and nameless, a nobody in a crowd—yet someone who believed everything she'd heard about Jesus. So she "came up behind him in the crowd and touched his garment. For she said, 'If I touch even his garments, I will be made well'" (vv. 27–28).

She was thinking, *I'm too embarrassed to let Him know I'm here. I'm too embarrassed to draw attention to myself and my condition in this crowd. But this Jesus is so awesome that even if I never get to talk with Him, even if He never acknowledges me, even if He never knows my name—even if all I can do is touch His clothes—I know He's so powerful that even that single touch will make me well.*

So she carried out her plan. She approached Him from the rear, sight unseen.

One of the other gospels tells us that it was the hem of His cloak that she touched. So she had to get down low—coming to Jesus in humble dependence, not arrogantly. Yet she also came with confidence and conviction. She was determined at all costs to draw near to Jesus and touch Him.

GRACE GREATER THAN LAW

Technically, what this woman did was a violation of the law because of her uncleanness. The stipulations in Leviticus did not allow a woman with a flow of blood to touch another person, or else that person would also become unclean. So to pull off her plan, she had to skip over the law.

How can we explain that? Very simple: Grace has always been greater than law. What she needed was grace, and that grace was there in the person of Jesus. The Bible says that "the law was given through Moses," but "grace and truth came through Jesus Christ" (John 1:17). The law was telling this woman to go away and not touch Jesus or anyone else; but grace was calling out, "Come close! I'm here for you!" The law said she was an outcast; grace was say-

Grace has always been greater than law.

■ ■ ■ ■ ■ ■ ■ ■ ■ ■ ■ ■ ■

ing, "There's room for you here; come take your place." The law said she was condemned; grace was saying, "Your condemnation is cancelled."

In the midst of her pain, and in spite of the high risk of major embarrassment, she quietly drew near and did what it took to get connected to the Author of grace.

WHEN JESUS ASKS A QUESTION

Once she finally got close enough to touch Him, two things happened "immediately."

First, a supernatural event occurred inwardly in her physical being. "And *immediately* the flow of blood dried up, and she felt in her body that she was healed of her disease" (Mark 5:29). She had been trying unsuccessfully to get cured for twelve years; now, having come to the perfect source of healing, she didn't have to wait even twelve minutes. She was healed in a single instant. And she knew it. She *experienced* it.

Second, her encounter elicited a response of full awareness from her Healer. "And Jesus, perceiving in himself that power had gone out from him, *immediately* turned about in the crowd and said, 'Who touched my garments?'" (v. 30).

Now, why did Jesus ask such a question?

That's what the disciples were wondering. They quickly pointed out the obvious: "You see the crowd pressing around you, and yet you say, 'Who touched me?'" (v. 31). Frankly, they didn't understand the question. The obvious truth of the matter was that a whole bunch of people had touched Him, because He was being pressed by the crowd.

I can tell you for sure that when Jesus asks anyone a question, it isn't because He's deficient in knowledge. His questions aren't for His benefit, but for ours. His questions are designed to awaken and stimulate our own understanding and to prepare us for His answers.

Jesus that day asked a singular question; the disciples gave a plural answer. Jesus wanted them to identify the *individual* who had touched Him; the disciples instead identified the crowd that was in His vicinity.

His questions aren't for His benefit, but for ours.

A Different Touch

Jesus knew power had gone forth from Him. He knew someone had touched Him—someone did it not as a celebrity-hound or a thrill-seeker, but with the touch of faith. "And he looked around to see who had done it" (5:32).

He was surrounded by a multitude that day; why didn't more people draw close enough to Him in faith to experience divine power coming forth from Jesus into their lives? All these folks were pressing in against Him; why did He recognize and acknowledge the touch of only one?

Because most of the multitude that day were there only to see a show. "A great crowd" was following Jesus to the home of Jairus to see what He would do with that rich man's dying daughter. They were eager to see another miracle.

But this bleeding woman wasn't interested in a show. She was interested only in the Person at the center of all the commotion. She knew who He really was, and she was determined to touch Him because of her desperate need. She wasn't satisfied merely to be part of a parade. Her touch was different than the crowd's touch. They were just pressing in; she wanted *Him.*

MAKING THE CONNECTION

Fundamentally, the other folks there that day didn't know who they were following. They didn't know who they were dealing with.

It reminds me of the time Michael Jordan went to Las Vegas to get married in one of those quickie wedding chapels. After the ceremony, the man who married the couple looked up at the groom. He commented on how tall he was, then asked, "Have you ever thought about playing basketball?"

That man just didn't understand who he was dealing with.

A lot of us are in the vicinity of Jesus, like the crowd was that day in Mark's Gospel, but we don't really understand who we're dealing with. We don't truly realize that He's the Son of the living God, God incarnate, Jesus the Christ. We don't really understand that when we draw near enough to touch Him by faith, the power that can flow out from Him is supernatural in its effect. It's the same divine power that can turn a valley-full of dry bones into a vast army of living, breathing soldiers for the Lord. It's the same divine enablement that can transform our lives. It's the same divine force that can turn our desperate issues into opportunities to display God's glory and might.

You can be in the vicinity of Jesus, you can be in the neighborhood, without really being someone who's touched Jesus and received His power to heal and refresh. Just because you're in the crowd doesn't mean you're making the connection.

Just because you're in the crowd doesn't mean you're making the connection.

■ ■ ■ ■ ■ ■ ■ ■ ■ ■ ■

FROM NOBODY TO SOMEBODY

Jesus wanted to know who had touched Him, and the disciples questioned the question. So Jesus looked around in the crowd to receive the answer, and He didn't have to wait. "The woman, knowing what had happened to her, came in fear and trembling and fell down before him and told him the whole truth" (5:33).

Her quick and full response shows us both the real purpose and the impact of Jesus' question. I want to help you look at this more carefully in later chapters of this book, but for now, just fix your attention on how Jesus responded to her: "Daughter, your faith has made you well; go in peace, and be healed of your disease" (v. 34).

After she fell before Him and testified what had happened, after her situation brought glory to Jesus, the result for her was *personal intimacy with Jesus.* He actually called her "daughter." Don't miss that. When we started this story, she had no name. Now she's gone from being nobody to being the daughter of Jesus. Suddenly, a totally new relationship has turned a nobody into someone special.

Jesus told this new daughter of His to "go in peace." This was *shalom* peace—the peace that in the Jewish mind means total well-being. It means all of life being put in proper perspective. It means having all of life's needs being abundantly met. Her medical issue had just been taken care of; now Jesus was telling her that He was taking care of *all* her issues—all because of her intimate relationship with Him.

This intimacy with Him is all that any of us really needs. I love what God tells us in Jeremiah 9:23–24: "Let not the wise man boast in his wisdom, let not the mighty man boast in his might, let not the rich man boast in his riches, but let him who boasts boast in this, that he understands and knows me." If you can't brag about your intimacy with the Lord, then you really don't have much to talk about.

For All Your Issues

Few of us have circumstances as numerous and as severely difficult as those faced by the woman in Mark 5 before she encountered Jesus. But though we can't identify with *all* her issues, most of us can identify with one or two of them. We face physical problems that doctors haven't been able to resolve. Or we're in financial trauma. Or there are psychological issues that mess with our mind and cause embarrassment or emotional pain. Or we have social issues that bring broken fellowship, broken relationships, and we aren't getting as close to people as we need. Or we have spiritual issues that make us desperately in need of experiencing God's grace, desperately in need of hearing Him call us "My son" or "My daughter" and hearing Him say, "Go in peace."

What are your issues today? And how long have you been dealing with those issues? Perhaps they go back even longer than twelve years.

Whatever the issue is…I want you to know that there's plenty of God's grace to address it, as you draw near to Him in intimacy.

are you paying the price?

■ If you've ridden on a passenger train, have you checked out the prices of food service? The cost for a meal on a train is staggering. I traveled by rail not long ago and discovered it took close to fifteen dollars to buy what would normally cost three dollars at McDonald's.

The reason for this is simple: They know you aren't going anywhere else. If you're going to eat, they're the only game in town. So they control the price. And if you're hungry enough, you'll pay it.

ALWAYS A SACRIFICE

In your hunger for the passion and power God offers through His Spirit, what price you are willing to pay? After all, He really is the only game in town.

Or let me put it another way: What is your pursuit of God costing you? Because in case you didn't know it, all biblical worship, all service of God, all encounter with God involves a sacrifice.

When you're passionate about something,
you'll pick up the tab.

It was unknown in the Old Testament to approach God without some sacrifice. There was expense involved in entering His presence. I like the way David put it: "I will not offer burnt offerings to the LORD my God that cost me nothing" (2 Samuel 24:24). He understood that there's a price tag involved in worship—not because you're buying something from God, because that would nullify grace. It was rather because you recognize the worth of the God whom you worship. And when you're passionate about something, you'll pick up the tab.

As you prepare yourself for the mighty miracle of renewal God wants to accomplish in your life, as you continue your pilgrimage into His presence and to see His mighty hand at work in your life, the question I want to ask you next is this: Are you willing to pay the price?

Hunger Test

To help us understand that question and to see the truths and the principles involved, I want to take you back to the familiar story in Genesis about Abraham's sacrifice of Isaac.

That story makes it clear that God will test our hunger for Him by what we are willing to sacrifice. It's one thing to say you're hungry for God and for His presence and power and to be asking for it; it's another thing to be willing to *sacrifice* for it. But that's the one and only way I know for you to validate that you're truly as hungry for God as you say you are.

The Bible calls it a test.

Why does God test our hunger for Him? Because the passion of our lives must be for God and not merely for His blessings and gifts. God doesn't mind giving us blessings out of His hand as long as what we truly want is His heart. He's not interested in being our genie in a bottle. He's not interested in being our Santa Claus. He's not interested in being our cosmic bellhop, which is what most people use Him for. He's interested in responding to people who are in active pursuit of His heart and who'll make the appropriate sacrifice in order to experience it.

Testing Time Follows Blessing Time

The story of Abraham laying Isaac on the altar begins this way: "After these things God tested Abraham" (Genesis 22:1). Which leads us to wonder: "After *what* things?"

From the previous chapter we discover that this time of testing followed a time of blessing. Abraham had formed a peace treaty with Abimelech, ruler of the Philistines, and at the end of chapter 21 we see Abraham enjoying a wonderful worship time with God: "Abraham planted a tamarisk tree in Beersheba and called there on the name of the LORD, the Everlasting God" (21:33).

Isn't it amazing how often our times of prosperity and contentment can get interrupted by testings from God? And for the man Abraham, this particular interruption would be earth-shattering.

God called his name: "Abraham!"

He answered obediently and yieldingly: "Here am I."

Then God spoke these words: "Take your son, your only son Isaac, whom you love, and go to the land of Moriah, and offer him there as a burnt offering on one of the mountains of which I shall tell you" (22:2).

He was sending Abraham to Mount Moriah to worship Him, and in order to worship Him he would need to bring a sacrifice, and the sacrifice He asked for was Abraham's son. And not just his son, but his "only son." And not just his only son, but "Isaac, whom you love." Isaac, whose birth had been so clearly a miraculous gift from God.

There was nothing God could have asked for that could have rocked Abraham more than that.

GIVING UP THE FIRST AND THE BEST

Many of us wouldn't mind God testing us as long as it didn't involve something we valued so highly, something or someone that's one-of-a-kind for us, the only one like it we have, and something or someone we love. We want to say, "God, test me over something I hate, something I don't mind giving up." In other words, "Test me over my leftovers, Lord. Test me over stuff I'm not using anyway. Test me over things that don't matter to me."

That's why, in the area of giving, when God asks His people to give a tenth of their income, He asks them to give it off the top, not after they've seen whether they have any left over.

Only when you're tested in an area of
affection do you know who you really love.

■ ■ ■ ■ ■ ■ ■ ■ ■ ■ ■ ■

God asked Abraham to give Him the most precious thing in
His life. Why? Because only when you're tested in an area of affection do you know who you really love. It was true for Abraham in
Old Testament times, and it's true for us today as well. Jesus tells
us, "If anyone comes to me and does not hate his own father and
mother and wife and children and brothers and sisters, yes, and
even his own life, he cannot be my disciple" (Luke 14:26).
Everything else, and everyone else, must be second to God. Jesus
said, "Seek first the kingdom of God and his righteousness, and all
these things will be added to you" (Matthew 6:33).

What Your Heart Clings To

God asked Abraham for what was most valuable to Him. And you
and I will get hit by this kind of test as well, and it will involve a
severe cost.

I'm not talking about a headache. I'm not talking about being
irritated because the kids are misbehaving. I'm talking about
being called upon by God to offer back to Him something precious, something that grips your heartstrings, because it involves
your deepest affections. You're having to relinquish your heart's
ownership over something your heart does not want to part with.

It may involve a relationship that clearly isn't what God intends for you. Or it may involve a possession or a position He wants you to let go of. I don't know what it will be, but I can say with certainty that you will be tested on that which your heart clings to. I can guarantee it. He will test your willingness to sacrifice something that represents one of the most valuable things in your life, something that's as precious to you as Isaac was to Abraham.

Why does God do this? Why does He test us like this?

Because He's ready to take us to the next level. The test will take every bit of spiritual reserve we have to pass because He's ready to move us up to the next grade level in our journey of following Him and growing closer to Him.

THE QUESTION OF FAITH

In whatever God asks us to sacrifice, He'll be testing not only our willingness to sacrifice but also our faith.

His tests can come like an alarm clock early in the morning. That obnoxious sound calls you to get up even though you don't feel like it. It has interrupted one of your nicer dreams and interfered with the full eight hours of sleep you wanted. You don't want to get up at that particular time, but the alarm insists that it's time. And so, though you're perhaps aggravated and irritated, you force yourself out of bed and into the shower. No matter how you feel about it, you get up. You don't act on your feelings, but on something of higher value and importance than your feelings.

The question of faith is never the question of feelings.

■ ■ ■ ■ ■ ■ ■ ■ ■ ■ ■ ■

God's alarms often seem to go off in our lives at the wrong time. Both His timing and His methodologies seem to ring in the wrong way, and they don't feel right to us. But the question of faith is never the question of feelings. The question of faith is never, "How do I feel right now about what God has said to me?" That's never the question of faith; it's the question of feelings.

It's not that those feelings aren't real; it's not that we can easily dismiss them. They're very real. But faith means always acting like God is telling the truth. And once we do that, regardless of our feelings, then God can alter our feelings later. We have to trust Him to shake off our cobwebs of not wanting to do what He tells us to do, because if we obey in what He commands us, we can be assured that He'll eventually cause us to feel good about it.

MAKING NO SENSE

What God requested from Abraham made absolutely no sense. It wasn't something Abraham could figure out. It was a contradiction. God had already assured him that Isaac was His gift to him, and that through Isaac Abraham would be the father of many nations. "Through Isaac shall your offspring be named" (Genesis 21:12). But how could his son fulfill that role if God took his life at this time? Isaac probably was only in his teenage years at this point, and he was unmarried and had no children. It just didn't make sense. You can't engender "many nations" through a son who's dead.

When you face your own test from God, it very likely will not make sense. You'll wonder what in the world God is doing. *Why would He provide me with this house and now it's in danger of being foreclosed? Why would He supply me with this great job and now everything at work is falling apart? Why would He give me this relationship and then bring such heartache through it?*

It doesn't make sense to you because it's a test. And God may not explain much of it to you even if you ask Him. Because what He's testing is your faith, and the Lord's question in the test is always the same: "Do you love *me* more than these?" (John 21:15).

THE NEED FOR TRUST

If you're looking for logic when it comes to your testings from God—or practically any aspect of living the Christian life, for that matter—you'll find yourself often confused. "For my thoughts are not your thoughts, neither are your ways my ways, declares the LORD"; the gap between how He thinks and how we think is as vast "as the heavens are higher than the earth" (Isaiah 55:8–9).

So when it comes to your breakthrough, when it comes to seeing God accomplish what you need in your life, He may get you to take on new emptiness before He fills you up, even though that makes so little sense to us.

When God began His test of Abraham, He didn't give him full information. He told Abraham to sacrifice Isaac "on one of the mountains *of which I shall tell you*" (22:2). God wasn't giving him all the details up front. A lot of us would be more willing to take the test if we had all the information in advance and could see how this was going to wind up for us—then we could better decide whether we wanted to take this test. But God isn't offering that as an option. He's testing how much we trust *His* judgment, not our own.

FAST OBEDIENCE

Consider carefully how Abraham reacted to God's request: "So Abraham rose early in the morning" (22:3). I probably would have wanted to sleep late that day. I might have laid in bed and just moaned, "Woe is me. How can God ask this? How can God demand this?" I might have had a headache and couldn't set out till I'd had three cups of coffee.

But Abraham got up early. He was quick to respond to God. There was immediate obedience. He didn't understand God's request, but he neither argued with it nor procrastinated in fulfilling it.

Nor did he get sidetracked by trying to explain it to anybody else. Along with his son Isaac, Abraham took two servants with him on this journey, but he didn't reveal to them all the details of what God had told him to do. When he caught sight of the place God had directed him to, he simply said to his two servants, "Stay here with the donkey; I and the boy will go over there and worship and come again to you" (v. 5).

When God has you in the kind of test you can't understand, it may well be a situation that you can't begin to fully explain to anybody else. After all, if you can't comprehend it yourself, how would you even start in describing it to others? Sometimes you have to keep what God is doing close to your vest.

But observe well what Abraham *did* tell those servants. He said "I *and* the boy" would worship the Lord and then return. Worship for Abraham in this specific situation would mean obediently killing his son—yet Abraham stated that they *both* would return; he was saying, "We'll be back." Now that's a statement of faith.

THROWING IT BACK ON GOD

Then Isaac had a question for his father. "Behold, the fire and the wood, but where is the lamb for a burnt offering?" (22:7). Isaac didn't understand what was happening either.

Abraham answered with another statement of faith: "God will provide for himself the lamb for a burnt offering, my son" (v. 8). He was saying, "God knows best how to take care of this. I'm putting this one on God, because it's beyond me." That's all he could say. That's all the information he could give. But it was the truth, and it was enough. He threw it all back on God, because Abraham was in a situation that goes way beyond human perception. It stretched beyond what you can see with your eyes or hear with your ears or figure out with your mind.

Sometimes our hour of testing will simply go beyond a matter of counseling, and beyond talking to your friends, and beyond trying to read books or attending conferences and seminars to find help. It just exceeds and surpasses all of that. God is doing something unique with you, and He Himself has to provide what you need. It has to come directly from Him.

GOD IS ABLE

We find out more information about what was happening here in Abraham's mind and heart by turning to the Spirit's inspired words in the New Testament:

> By faith Abraham, when he was tested, offered up Isaac, and he who had received the promises was in the act of offering up his only son, of whom it was said, 'Through Isaac shall your offspring be named.' He considered that God was able even to raise him from the dead, from which, figuratively speaking, he did receive him back. (Hebrews 11:17–19)

He recognized God's awesome ability to do the impossible.

That's why Abraham said what he did to his servants about coming back to them with Isaac. Abraham thought he had a resurrection on his hands. He knew God had the power to do exactly that, and that was the only solution he could see to this test God was taking him through.

Have you ever taken a written examination and come to a question that seemed to come out of nowhere? You were sure it didn't belong on the test. You were sure this particular material simply wasn't in the book. The instructor never covered it. To you, it was simply a question with no answer.

God never gives a test for which there's no answer.

■ ■ ■ ■ ■ ■ ■ ■ ■ ■ ■ ■ ■

God never gives a test for which there's no answer, but He does give tests where you don't have the answer in advance. You have to simply believe that God is able, just as Abraham believed that God could raise Isaac from the dead. He had no idea how it could work, but he didn't have to know. He trusted that God was able.

ALWAYS AN ALTAR

God was testing Abraham's willingness to let go of that which mattered most to him, and he was testing Abraham's faith. And when this trial came to a climax, we see that this kind of testing always occurs in the context of sacrificial worship.

"When they came to the place of which God had told him, Abraham built the altar there" (22:9). Abraham built an altar—a place of sacrificial worship—and laid his son Isaac upon it.

Is there something God wants you now to put on the altar? If you, like Abraham, are in the middle of a test that you can't figure out, then the one place you want to be is at worship. Approach His heavenly altar where the sacrifice of His Son, Jesus, has opened the way for you into the presence of God. Worship the Lamb and worship God on His throne, even though you don't understand what He's taking you through. Worship even though you can't begin to figure it out. Follow through in sacrificial worship.

And there at the altar God will show you His way. He'll come through for you.

Going All the Way

After building his altar, Abraham at that point could have said, "God, I've obeyed You. I got up early to leave home. I walked all this way and came to this mountain. And I've built an altar. Now that's as far as I'm going."

But once the altar was built, heaven was still silent. Because God's command to Abraham was not simply to get up early or to climb the mountain or to build an altar. His command to Abraham was to offer his son Isaac as a sacrifice. And that was not yet done.

Maybe you've approached God in worship, but you're still waiting for Him to come through. The reason may well be that you haven't finished the test. You have to go all the way. And when you go all the way, that's when it hurts. Worship the Lord all the way, even when it hurts.

That's what Abraham did. Remember that Abraham *loved* his son. He loved him as much as you or I have ever loved anyone. But after he built his altar, he didn't stop there. He "laid the wood in order and bound Isaac his son and laid him on the altar, on top of the wood. Then Abraham reached out his hand and took the knife to slaughter his son" (22:9–10).

And that knife was piercing Abraham's own heart even more than it could ever pierce his son's body.

Transfer of Ownership

Only then did God intervene: "But the angel of the LORD called to him from heaven and said, 'Abraham, Abraham!' And he said,

'Here am I'" (22:11). It was the same ready-and-willing servant's response that Abraham gave when this trial first began.

But the instructions God had for him today were so much different: "Do not lay your hand on the boy or do anything to him, for now I know that you fear God, seeing you have not withheld your son, your only son, from me" (vv. 11–12). Look again at that last sentence: "You have not withheld your only son...*from me.*" In Abraham's heart, ownership of his son had been fully transferred. And the God of resurrection power was now free to keep Isaac alive and to fulfill through his life his promises to Abraham.

Abraham now knew far more than he ever had about his faith—and also about his God.

Why does God send us through experiences like this? Because those tests reveal to us where we stand. They let us know whether we really love Him as much as we say we do in our songs and our prayers.

The Rewards Always Outweigh the Sacrifice

As it ended up, the reward Abraham received for this act of sacrificial worship was far greater than the cost of the sacrifice he offered.

Listen carefully to all that Abraham was promised that day as he embraced his son in his arms and helped him down from the altar:

> "By myself I have sworn, declares the LORD, because you
> have done this and have not withheld your son, your only
> son, I will surely bless you, and I will surely multiply your

offspring as the stars of heaven and as the sand that is on the seashore. And your offspring shall possess the gate of his enemies, and in your offspring shall all the nations of the earth be blessed, because you have obeyed my voice." (22:16–18)

Imagine what Abraham was thinking that night—as he sat with his son Isaac in their encampment on the journey home—and they looked up together at the uncountable stars. That's how many sons and daughters Abraham would have through Isaac. Through Isaac, Abraham would become a blessing to every nation on earth. Abraham could only conclude that God's rewards infinitely surpassed the sacrifices He had required.

The same is true for us. God will reward our passion for Him in a way that's far greater than any sacrifice He asks for. The test will be hard—but the reward will more than compensate for the pain.

I don't know how your breakthrough from God is going to come to you. I can't say how He'll do it. All I know is, if you've come into His presence in sacrificial worship and you've given Him the experience of your passion and your love, then what He will do for you will far outstrip anything you can imagine giving up.

God's rewards infinitely surpass the sacrifices He requires.

■ ■ ■ ■ ■ ■ ■ ■ ■ ■ ■ ■

The Lord Will Provide

Abraham passed his test with flying honors. That's why he's in the hall of faith in Hebrews 11.

After the passing the test, he renamed that hilltop where he'd offered Isaac: "Abraham called the name of that place, 'The LORD will provide'"—*Jehovah Jireh.* It was a place Abraham would always remember and a lesson he would always remember: God provides (22:14).

As you hear those words, I know the question you're asking now regarding your own situation: Exactly *how* will God provide for me?

I don't have the slightest idea. I wish I could help you, but God has not consulted me on it. I don't have detailed answers for your trial and your need. But I want to ask you this: Have you been to the altar with sacrifice? It's only there that you'll discover personally the truth that God will always come through for you.

And when He finally gives you that breakthrough, rename that place and that experience in your memory. Give it the name *Jehovah Jireh*—"The Lord will provide."

Take the Knife

Sooner or later, God asks every believer to take a knife to something. It could be a financial matter, or it could be a relationship, or it could be something else. I don't know what it will be for you. But He's going to ask you to trust Him. He's going to ask if you're willing to kill it—if you love Him enough to make the sacrifice.

He may take it from you. Or He may, as He did with Abraham, entrust it back into your stewardship, though you'll never think of it in the same way again.

Whatever it is...are you willing to pay the price?

are YOU Enduring?

■ You've heard the words and have probably even spoken them yourself: "God will never give us more than we can bear." But have you ever sensed that this statement just isn't true?

That's because it isn't.

Now, it is true in a certain way. We know it's accurate regarding temptation to sin, because the Scriptures say, "God is faithful, and he will not let you be tempted beyond your ability, but with the temptation he will also provide the way of escape, that you may be able to endure it" (1 Corinthians 10:13). When you fall into sin, it's never because the temptation was unbearable, but because you chose not to take the way of escape God provided.

However, when it comes to life's difficulties and stresses and burdens, the occasions will indeed come when God puts more on you than you can bear. Those are the times when He wants to break you. He wants to bring you to brokenness, to bring you to the end of your own resources, so you'll say, "I can't."

Then God says, "Gotcha." He has you where He wants you. God breaks us, and this is good.

ONLY IN THE PAIN

That's a big part of why Paul said that he wanted to share in the sufferings of Christ (Philippians 3:10). There's an experience of God that we can get in no other way than through the pain He allows in our lives. And when you wonder why He allows the pain to last so long, it's because He's trying to take you deeper.

That's why we're told, "Beloved, do not be surprised at the fiery trial when it comes upon you to test you, as though something strange were happening to you. But rejoice insofar as you share Christ's sufferings, that you may also rejoice and be glad when his glory is revealed" (1 Peter 4:12–13). If you want to see and enjoy His glory, you must first share in His sufferings. Those sufferings help us recognize our weakness and our insufficiency so we can learn to endure them with *His* strength instead of our own.

By His strength, we *can* endure.

So my next question is this: Are you doing it? Are you enduring, even when you face more than you can bear?

Let me help you discover from God's Word how to do exactly that.

He allows the pain to last so long because He's trying to take you deeper.

■ ■ ■ ■ ■ ■ ■ ■ ■ ■ ■ ■

A MAN STRICKEN WITH DRYNESS

Recall with me again the situation of hopeless despair that characterized the people of God in Ezekiel's day. I want us to quickly look at a couple of other passages that share some commonalities with Ezekiel 37, and which shed additional light for us on the spiritual renewal we're longing for and waiting for.

One of the chapters in the Psalms that closely echoes the hopelessness in Ezekiel's day is Psalm 42. First of all there's dryness there. The psalm begins with these familiar words: "As a deer pants for flowing streams, so pants my soul for you, O God. My soul thirsts for God, for the living God" (vv. 1–2). This man recognizes his dryness and seeks the refreshment only God provides.

In his utter need, he could have easily identified with those parched bones in the valley in Ezekiel's vision. And in fact, as the people in Ezekiel 37 lamented, "Our bones are dried up," so also the psalmist cries out about "a deadly wound in my bones" (v. 10). His spiritual dryness goes deep, and it hurts.

The people in Ezekiel's day came to the anguished conclusion, "Our hope is cut off." In a similar way the psalmist keeps aiming for hope, but he grieves that his soul is "cast down" and "in turmoil within me" (v. 5). The reality of his situation brings him disillusionment and despair, and he feels abandoned by God: "I say to God, my rock: 'Why have you forgotten me?'" (v. 9).

If the truth were told, many of us feel forsaken by God as well. We're disappointed with Him. If He truly cares about us, why must we wait so long for Him to respond?

OUT OF REACH

The man in Psalm 42 finds himself in trouble and despair, and it's not because he doesn't have a strong spiritual background and history. In fact, it's those who have known God for the longest time who seem most likely at one time or another to experience a profound sense of abandonment by God.

If you've been saved for any length of time and you've had the extended spiritual experience of feeling close to Him, then you also know what it means to feel like God has gone away on a long-distance vacation and not informed you where He was going. If you've never felt the aching distance of God, then you probably haven't walked near to Him for very long.

What do you do when God is nowhere to be found? How in the world is it possible to endure such a thing? You sense that you don't sense Him, especially when life's troubles pour in like a flood and He doesn't respond to your prayers. In fact, the harder you seek after Him, the further He seems to be.

If you haven't experienced all this yet...then just keep living, and you will.

MAJOR DEPRESSION AND SPIRITUAL STRUGGLE

The psalmist has observed a deer in desperate search of water, and he easily relates that to his own trouble. He recognizes how water sustains the physical life of a deer and how this creature will pursue it no matter the cost. In the same way, the psalmist knows that God sustains his life and that he must pursue Him until he finds Him. There is no other option.

This is major depression.

■ ■ ■ ■ ■ ■ ■ ■ ■ ■ ■ ■

He's in hot pursuit of God because life has done a number on him. This man is suffering emotionally. "My tears have been my food day and night," he says (42:3). He's crying all day and all night. This is major depression. It's so bad that tears are now his food. In other words, he can't eat because things are so bad. His appetite is gone.

His emotional state is despair, and despair means all hope is gone. There's no way out. You feel you've run the course of all your options and none of them has worked. That's when tears take over and rule. If you're crying when you don't want to cry, if you have to go to the restroom at work in order to shed tears privately so no one sees your pain, then you know of what the psalmist speaks.

He's also struggling spiritually because he feels that God is nowhere to be found. His soul feels a desperate thirst for God that isn't being satisfied, and he cries out, "When shall I come and appear before God?" (v. 2). That's a spiritual struggle. It's one thing to be in emotional despair; it's quite another to be in emotional despair and also not know where God is. That's double trouble.

It wasn't always like this. He remembers better days—"how I would go with the throng and lead them in procession to the house of God with glad shouts and songs of praise" (v. 4). Back then, he came to God joyfully. Now he comes with tears.

BOTH HEARTACHE AND HEADACHE

To this man, God seems so distant that even other people notice it about him. "They say to me continually, 'Where is your God?'" (42:3).

If you're a Christian worth your salt, then I'm sure you've been in a situation where you were defending God to unbelievers and yet inwardly you had some of the same questions as they were asking. While they're saying, "Where is God?" you're thinking, *Yes, where is He?*

The psalmist is struggling physically as well. As we noticed earlier, he feels "a deadly wound in my bones" (v. 10). When you struggle enough emotionally and spiritually, it can bring you down physically.

Have you ever been so depressed that the only place you wanted to be was in bed? Your situation not only gives you a heartache, it gives you a headache. Maybe you have to call in sick though the doctors can't find anything wrong. Or maybe you're really battling a severe physical ailment, a literal "deadly wound," yet the suffering is inextricably tied to your emotional and spiritual distress.

This man is also struggling relationally, because he's surrounded by those who added to his grief: "My adversaries taunt me, while they say to me continually, 'Where is your God?'" (v. 10). Maybe you have coworkers or neighbors or even family members who seem like that to you.

Both Heaven and Hell

So for the man who has written these words recorded for us in Psalm 42, his life at this point is not a happy sight. That's one reason I love the Bible, because it doesn't paint a glossy picture of life—so neither will I. The fact is, life isn't always sweet. The Christian life on earth isn't all joy and bliss. That's heaven. But earth is a mixture of heaven and hell.

Reading this psalm, and many other psalms like it, you have to conclude that either the psalmist is carnal and his carnality is the cause of his misery, or else maybe he's not carnal, but rather he's a spiritual man who's living honestly in a real world.

This man is struggling with real questions, just like the writer of Psalm 73 was authentically struggling when he said that seeing the prosperity of the wicked caused him to envy them as well as to doubt the value of obeying God. If you've never felt the same way, then you're not living in the real world. And if I were to dare say that you wouldn't have such questions if you were only more spiritual, then I wouldn't be a true minister of the Lord. Because the Bible is full of these kinds of issues. It's full of the question, "Where is God?"

God wants you to be hungering.

■ ■ ■ ■ ■ ■ ■ ■ ■ ■ ■

THE HIGHER REALITY

But the man in Psalm 42 is doing more than recognizing honestly the reality around him. He's also persevering in the honest pursuit of true spiritual reality, which is the higher reality.

As he thinks of the thirsty deer panting after water, he says, "So pants my soul"—for what?—"for *you, O God*" (v. 1). Not for God's blessings or His gifts, but for God Himself.

Could it be that God wants you to be hungering and thirsting more for Him and less for a solution to your problem or an answer to your question or a provision for your need? Unwanted circumstances bring us despair, and we want a change right now, when maybe all God is offering us is Himself.

If God isn't answering your prayer about your situation, maybe you should change the focus of your prayer. Tell God honestly, "What I really want is You, and what I'll take is You, even if You don't change my circumstances. I'll still take You, no matter what." And you endure in pursuing God in the midst of a struggle that's emotionally, spiritually, relationally, and physically painful.

> Maybe all God is offering us is Himself.

. . . .

GETTING IN GOD'S FACE

As this man perseveres in pursuing God's reality while also recognizing honestly his own struggles, it appears in this psalm that he's on an emotional seesaw. He goes back and forth from despair to hope, from disturbance to peace. He's up and down. He fluctuates between sobs and songs, confidence and collapse, fear and faith.

He's in a real conflict, a real wrestling match.

One moment he's saying, "By day the LORD commands his steadfast love, and at night his song is with me, a prayer to the God of my life" (42:8).

But in the very next line he's asking God, "Why have you forgotten me?" It's an honest question and a painful question. It isn't a now-I-lay-me-down-to-sleep prayer, but a getting-in-God's-face prayer. This man is desperate.

But he hasn't given up.

Choosing to Remember

In the middle of this psalm, he tells God, "My soul is cast down within me; therefore *I remember you*" (v. 6). In the middle of his desperation, by perseverance and endurance, he chooses to remember God.

That's why it's important to have a history with God in the good times so you don't forget Him in the bad times. If life with God for you is good now, if He's brought gladness to your heart through a new blessing, then enjoy it to the max and either write down an account of it that you can return to later, or put that account in the memory bank of your mind—because you're going to need that story one day. You'll need to be able to look back and see the footsteps of God's grace. Living in the past isn't always good, but when it comes to remembering God's blessings when you're going through hard times, it *is* good.

We read in the Old Testament how they were always rehearsing what God did. Hundreds of years later they're still telling the next generation about how their forefathers in Egypt were caught between Pharaoh and the Red Sea, and God opened up a roadway in the waters, brought them through, and then led them onward through the wilderness, and how He didn't allow their clothes or their sandals to wear out, and how He provided them with manna from heaven to eat.

For the same reason, mothers and fathers today need to rehearse with their children the footsteps of God in their lives. They need to keep remembering the victories God gave them in the tough times in the past, because there'll be more tough times ahead.

That's why the man in Psalm 42 deliberately directs his mind to what God has done for him before. So that at the end of the psalm, though he must ask once more, "Why are you cast down, O my soul, and why are you in turmoil within me?" yet he can also tell himself with confidence, "Hope in God; for I shall again praise him, my salvation and my God" (v. 11). He knows that when God seems to be doing nothing, that's when He's usually doing His best work.

THERE WILL BE DARKNESS

This man's endurance means trusting God in the shadows and the gloom. He's saying, "In the midst of the darkness I have determined to hope in God."

Sometimes that's what you and I have to do as well. Yes, I know it's not the testimony we prefer. We'd rather talk about glowing miracles of how God came through, and there's a place for that. We want to be able to testify about new blessings and breakthroughs, and there's certainly an appropriate time for such celebration. But that's not the total picture. There are also times when it's dark and stays dark, and any version of Christianity that argues with that is not the truth, the whole truth, and nothing but the truth so help you God.

There'll be stress, crisis, persecution, and suffering. None of us would choose those times, none of us likes a bad day, none of us wants agony and affliction, and only a fool goes looking for it. But if you're alive and you're a Christian, you'll run into it.

It's been said that the words and value of your Christian faith is like a tea bag—you only see how strong it is when it's placed in hot water. It's easy to love God when all is well, but the proof of your love is when all is not well—when the challenges of life condense upon you, and you choose to love and remember Him anyway.

Yes, it gets dark sometimes. And prayer can be so difficult when it's dark and God seems distant. When God seems near you can pray all day long; you can kick in easy with God when He's up close. But when you need Him most, He's nowhere to be found, then it's tough to pray; it's daunting to carry on an in-depth conversation when it seems like nobody's on the other end.

But the truth could be that only when you're in such darkness and despair are you really ready to pray. Because only then are you're truly prepared to tell God the full truth about the depth of your need.

Prayer can be so difficult when it's dark and God seems so distant.

STUCK ON HOLD

When we're locked in that darkness, and we're looking for God's breakthrough day after day and it never seems any closer, and the burdens grow heavier, and the darkness deepens—that's when the waiting gets so tiresome and oppressive.

Sometimes we think the waiting wouldn't be so bad if we could just know a date and a time when it would end. Maybe then it would be easier to hold out. But when we pray about it, it's like we've telephoned God and He's pressed the hold button on the other end of the line, and hasn't let you know when He's coming back to the phone. You feel you've been forgotten.

But to help us endure in those situations God has given us special encouragement throughout His Word. I find it especially in a passage from Isaiah that addresses the same kind of hopelessness the people of God were experiencing in Ezekiel's day.

In Isaiah's time, God was hearing this complaint from so many hearts and voices: "My way is hidden from the LORD, and my right is disregarded by my God" (40:27). Or in other words, "It's not fair!"

God hears that complaint from many of us as well. "It's not fair for them to treat me this way at work. It's not fair for me to stay single this long. It's not fair that my child (or my husband or my wife) treats me this way. God, it's not fair that the breakthrough I've prayed for hasn't come yet." We feel that what is rightly due us has escaped the notice of God.

It's not that we're atheists doubting the existence of God. We're raising a much more practical question: Since I *know* God exists, why am I still waiting for His help and support and intervention in my life?

Singing the Blues

You can always tell when people are tired of waiting. They stop singing the gospel and start singing the blues. The blues as a music genre developed as the flip side of the gospel. The gospel was hope in God; the blues was the despondency of man.

If you've forgotten the gospel and gone to singing the blues, it's probably because you're tired of waiting.

To counter that tiredness, some people develop harmful

dependencies to prop them up. It could be alcohol or drugs or any number of things, but whatever it is, they turn to it to help them forget how long they've been waiting on God. They turn to some artificial experience to hype them up so they can simply go on for another day.

So often we come to the tragically mistaken conclusion that if God is silent, He must also be still. If we can't see Him doing something, He must be doing nothing. And sometimes when you wait and wait and wait, panic sets in. We lose control and make tragic mistakes.

INTO GOD'S CHARACTER

What does God's Word through the prophet Isaiah have to say to His people who feel so devastated by extended waiting?

Isaiah's message is that if you're waiting, if you feel you've been put on hold by God, then God has an invitation for you. He doesn't invite you to a new experience or a new thrill; what He first of all invites you into is a better view of His character.

Isaiah says, "Have you not known? Have you not heard? The LORD is the everlasting God, the Creator of the ends of the earth. He does not faint or grow weary; his understanding is unsearchable" (40:28).

God first of all invites you into a better view of His character.

▪ ▪ ▪ ▪ ▪ ▪ ▪ ▪ ▪ ▪ ▪

He says that in the context of our waiting, we must come to know the character of God. He reminds us of this because when we have to wait, it's so easy to forget what God is like. When you're waiting and all He seems to send your way are difficult circumstances and His own silence, that's when you must turn to what you know about God as the basis of your waiting.

He's "the everlasting God." He doesn't look at our clocks and watches and calendars to determine His plan. Time is different for Him than it is for us.

And He's "the creator of the ends of the earth," the creator of absolutely all things. As Creator, He has the ability to do anything He wants, whenever He chooses to do it, and without having to obtain any raw materials to get it done. He created this world out of nothing, with His own intention and Word, and He can also create our breakthroughs and our spiritual renewals out of nothing except His own intention and Word.

What's also true about Him is this: "He does not faint or grow weary." He never tires. He's never napping on us. He's never zoned out. Therefore He hasn't forgotten you; He hasn't overlooked your situation. He's fully aware of all the facts in your case, and He carefully notes all your feelings.

"His understanding is unsearchable." In other words, you can't figure God out, and you'll get a headache trying. There's no way in the world we can figure out the Unfigure-outable One. So don't get bent out of shape because He seems to be operating silently. You have no idea what in the world He's doing. You don't know why He's taking so long, and you're wasting your time if you try to uncover all the details of the delay. His understanding cannot be uncovered. That's what makes Him God.

STRENGTH TO THE WEARY

How then are we supposed to make it through our trial when we can't fathom what He's up to and when what seems right for us isn't coming our direction?

Here's how: "He gives power to the faint, and to him who has no might he increases strength" (40:29). To those who are weary and exhausted and about to fall, God extends energy and capacity.

God hasn't told me when or how His specific breakthrough for you is going to come, or even whether it's going to come. But there's something He *has* told me that I can pass on to you: While you're waiting for Him, He'll replenish you with new strength. He gives vigor and vitality to those whose get-up-and-go has gotten up and gone.

IT'S A GIFT

And notice this especially: Isaiah says that He *gives* this power and strength. You don't have to earn it. You don't have to work for it. It's His gift to those who are weary. The only qualification you need to receive this new strength while you wait is to be weary or weak.

You may ask, "Why don't I have that new strength yet? Why aren't I experiencing it already?" It may be because you're not truly weary—you're still trying to make it on your own strength, in the flesh. You're still manipulating, still maneuvering.

To be weary and fainting is to come to the end of your resources and your tactics and your assumptions. It means crying "Uncle!" It's saying to God, "If You don't take over, I won't make it."

God wants you in a totally dependent position. You can either place yourself there voluntarily or be forced into it.

For Young and Old, Weak and Strong

This weariness isn't a factor of how old you are. Even those among us who are the youngest and the strongest and the best-conditioned cannot get along in the Christian life without the new strength God provides. "Even youths shall faint and be weary, and young men shall fall exhausted" (40:30).

There are some who say in their trials, "Oh, if I were only twenty years younger, I could handle this." But God knows that isn't true. Even the young can get so worn out with life that they're ready to quit, ready even to commit suicide.

Every week I hear from people who are ready to throw in the towel. They're tired of their circumstances, tired of their marriages, tired of their work, tired of their lives. And they say, "If I don't have something quick from God that will give me a new filling, I know I can't make it. I'm just so *tired* of it all."

If that sounds only too familiar, then God's promise in verse 31 is for you: "They who wait for the LORD shall renew their strength; they shall mount up with wings like eagles; they shall run and not be weary; they shall walk and not faint."

God's renewal of strength is yours, no matter how tired you are.

■ ■ ■ ■ ■ ■ ■ ■ ■ ■ ■ ■

That's a promise you can bank on. God's renewal of strength is yours, no matter how tired you are. It's a renewal that means mounting up with wings like eagles. It's a renewal that means running ahead tirelessly and walking forward on your journey without weakening.

This kind of waiting for the Lord means looking to Him in the midst of your situation. It means to keep trusting even when there are difficulties. It means living and thinking and hoping in a Godward direction even though your circumstances haven't changed. It means believing God when believing God is the last thing you want to do.

Filling Up the Time

Finally, don't forget that waiting always involves time—there's no way around that. And it's true about waiting for God as well.

What are you supposed to do with that time?

Waiting on the Lord doesn't mean you sit in a corner and do nothing. Waiting on the Lord means you're so confident in Him and in His eventual breakthrough on your behalf that you proceed with *routine faithfulness* in all of life. You maintain your faithfulness to Him and to your God-given responsibilities even though life's daily details are mundane, frustrating, irritating, even depressing.

You do it because you understand that He can interrupt your life at any time. I can't tell you when—but that's what waiting is all about.

Waiting for the Lord means *not* going outside of the Lord to fix your situation yourself. The moment you go outside the Lord—outside His divinely ordained circumstances or outside His biblical guidelines—in order to work things out yourself, you're no longer waiting on Him. *He* has to be what you're waiting for, and nothing else. He's got to be the subject of your wait.

That's why God will often let our weariness increase until He finally becomes our only way out. He's waiting for us to discover that the battle is the Lord's. He's waiting for us to get caught between Pharaoh's army and the Red Sea so that all other options are gone and all we can do is stand back and watch the salvation of the Lord. He's waiting for us to be like David before Goliath, discarding Saul's armor because it doesn't fit and instead using only God's honor and God's Word and God's weapons to fight the giant before us.

Now, don't get me wrong. Waiting on the Lord doesn't mean ignoring human resources. It simply means that we use them only to the degree that God allows it. We don't step outside of His mechanisms, even when our back is against the wall.

An Updraft and a Second Wind

By waiting on the Lord, we exchange our weakness for His strength. We'll fly as the greatest birds fly—we "mount up with wings like eagles" (40:31). He becomes the wind beneath us, lifting us up so we can soar above the circumstances rather than live underneath them.

He lifts us higher than we ever thought possible.

■ ■ ■ ■ ■ ■ ■ ■ ■ ■ ■ ■ ■

It's that updraft of the Spirit that we looked at earlier. He updrafts us emotionally, psychologically, and spiritually. He lifts us higher than we ever expected to be, higher than we ever thought possible. He constantly brings us the right encouragement at the right time, the right current of air at the right time to keep us aloft. It seems to come out of nowhere; God just shows up.

In this passage, Isaiah gives us yet another encouraging picture of this renewal: God promises that we'll "run and not be weary." We get our second wind, even as we're striding along, racing down the path He's set before us. We hardly even think about running anymore; it seems effortless.

Even when the time for slower plodding comes, the time for walking, the time when very long distances must be covered—even then we "shall walk and not faint." We'll keep going. He keeps supplying the energy so that we know we'll make it. We won't give up.

BE STRONG AND COURAGEOUS...AND WAIT

David tells us, "Wait for the LORD; be strong, and let your heart take courage; wait for the LORD!" (Psalm 27:14).

I don't know what it is exactly that you're waiting on from the Lord. And I don't know how long you'll have to wait for it. But I do know God will supply everything you need to endure for as long as you must as you wait for Him.

Those who wait on the Lord receive a new capacity to keep going. He may give you the wings to lift you out of your discouraging circumstances and to leave them far behind. Or He may give you a fresh sense of His presence there alongside you as you journey on the weary road. Whatever it is, His promise is to keep providing you with a fresh new ability and vitality to keep on enduring.

are YOU worshiping?

In photography, the best work happens in a darkroom. When the lights are out, that's where the real development occurs. It's in the darkroom where negatives are turned into positives.

God so often brings our lives into the darkroom. What does He expect from us there? It may seem illogical and impossible, but what He really wants from us in the darkness is our worship. That kind of response says so much about us.

Worship comes easy when it's high noon in your life and the sun of circumstances is shining brightly—when your health is good, the money's flowing, and relationships are smooth and rewarding. But, in the darkroom of pain and problems and pressures, that's another story.

OUT IN THE OPEN

Return with me for a moment to that day with Jesus when the woman who was bleeding approached Him and found instantaneous healing for her affliction.

This woman had been prepared both to sneak in and to sneak out. She didn't want to be seen. She didn't want to be noticed. But Jesus didn't let her get her blessing and then quietly slip out. In the midst of that noisy crowd, Jesus loudly asked, "Who touched my garments?" (Mark 5:30). He'd experienced a release of power from His body into the body of someone who had touched Him in a way that nobody else was touching Him that day. And He wanted a public encounter with this person.

Imagine how this woman felt. On one hand, there would be the complete elation of experiencing instant and total release from an illness that had held her in bondage for twelve years. That illness had caused her to live a hidden life, and she wasn't accustomed to being recognized in public, nor did she desire it. But now she faced the incomparable awesomeness of being personally summoned to step forward by the Son of God—and to do it publicly, in the midst of a large crowd.

> How easy it would have been to hurry off and not turn back.

How easy it would have been for her to hurry off and not turn back. "But the woman, knowing what had happened to her, came in fear and trembling and fell down before him and told him the whole truth" (v. 33).

She fell down at the feet of her Healer and her Lord. She *worshiped*. And only then did she receive the Savior's full and lasting blessing from His own lips: "Daughter, your faith has made you well; go in peace, and be healed of your disease" (v. 34).

To be hungry for the Lord and to be asking and waiting for His miracle of renewal of passion and fervency and fire in your life—to be drawing near to Him, with willingness to pay whatever cost is involved and with full determination to endure—all this will culminate in authentic adoration and reverence and devotion for the Lord.

So in our journey in this book toward the discovery of His renewal, my next question for you is this: Are you worshiping Him?

DOWN IN A DUNGEON

To help us out with that question, step with me into a dungeon of darkness. We're there with Paul and Silas in Acts 16 at the end of a bad day—bad in the extreme. Proclaiming the gospel in Philippi had gotten them into deep trouble earlier that day. They'd been attacked by a mob, stripped naked, beaten with rods, then thrown "into the inner prison"—better known as a dungeon. Their jails weren't like our jails today. Dungeons were dark, dreary, and dirty.

Down there, things got even worse for them. Their legs were spread wide and their feet were fastened into stocks. They can't move or go anywhere, even for the purposes of bodily elimination. So this is not a pleasant place to be.

These men are suffering because of their testimony, because they've been following Christ. And Christ has brought them here.

What do we find these men doing next? You remember the story: "About midnight Paul and Silas were praying and singing hymns to God" (v. 25). They were worshiping and rejoicing.

ALWAYS REJOICING

We all like to praise God in the good times, and we ought to. "They hired me for that new position, praise God!"—nothing wrong with that. "More money, Hallelujah"—nothing wrong with that. "The doctor says it's not cancer, and I'm praising the Lord"—nothing wrong with that. Those are all good reasons to bless the Lord. When God is bringing breakthroughs, those are easy times to praise Him.

But what do you do when everything's collapsing?

The Paul who sang hymns to God in the Philippian dungeon is the same Paul who later wrote to the Philippian church, "Rejoice in the Lord *always;* again I will say, Rejoice" (Philippians 4:4). And "always" means even in the depths of a dungeon, even in the depths of the night.

MIDNIGHT MADNESS

It was "about midnight," the Scripture tells us, when Paul and Silas were singing and praying in that prison. Midnight is when it's dark. Spiritually, emotionally, and psychologically, the darkness of midnight can come for us at any time.

Midnight is when you're discouraged. Midnight is when you're depressed. Midnight is when things have collapsed on you and there's no way out. Midnight is when you're expecting God to do one thing and He does something else that you don't like. Midnight is when you're trying to do right and everything goes wrong. Midnight is when you've got what you don't want, or you want what you don't have.

W hen life just isn't fair—that's midnight.

■ ■ ■ ■ ■ ■ ■ ■ ■ ■ ■ ■

When life just isn't fair—that's midnight.

It's when you do your best and you get the worst. It's when you're standing up for God, but it looks like the devil is winning. It's when you're trusting God for victory and you get defeat. It's when Satan and circumstances are beating you black and blue.

It's midnight when you've earned the promotion, but the next guy has politicked his way to the top and gotten it instead. It's midnight when you face family problems you can't resolve. It's midnight when your children are rebellious and won't come home. It's midnight when your finances aren't working out like they're supposed to. It's midnight when the doctor tells you, "The test results are in and they don't look good."

Midnight is when there's no sunshine. There's no light to encourage you. At midnight, you're thinking you don't know how you can make it till the dawn. Midnight is when you want to swear and curse—and maybe you do exactly that, or maybe you're too scared to.

There are so many questions at midnight, and so little rest. Midnight keeps you thinking and tossing and turning. It keeps you asking why. Why me? Why us? Why this? Why now? At midnight you've got questions, and you want answers.

NO ESCAPE

Nobody escapes midnight, no matter how good and spiritual you are. Jesus said, "In the world you will have tribulation" (John 16:33). Paul was the great apostle, but even he had to admit to being "afflicted in every way" (2 Corinthians 4:8). This ordeal in the Philippian prison was only a fraction of the hardships he had to endure, though he deserved them as little as anyone.

So the hour of midnight circles around for all of us. And if it's not here for you now, be assured that it's coming soon.

When it comes, how you respond to it is the ultimate proof of what you think about God. It's the supreme test of what you really believe, because anybody can get their praise on at daylight when everything's going right. But God wants your praise in both daylight and darkness so you can echo what the psalmist said: "By day the LORD commands his steadfast love, and at night his song is with me, a prayer to the God of my life" (Psalm 42:8).

It was midnight for Paul and Silas—but they had God's song rising up from within them, as a prayer to the God of life. When things grew dark, their praise grew as well.

GOD IS STILL GOD

How was that possible? How can someone actually praise God in a midnight as dark as theirs was? In fact, how can God expect anyone to praise Him in the darkness?

Let me say first of all that if you aren't used to praising at daylight, it is going to be rough trying to come up with something at midnight! If you don't know how to reach heaven when things are good, it's for sure going to seem an impossible distance away when things are bad!

But Paul and Silas did it. Why? It was dark in that innermost prison, and smelly, and they were lonely and shackled and bruised and bleeding. How could they praise God in those circumstances?

I know of only one reason. You praise God at midnight—when your world's collapsed, when nothing's fair, when it's all bad and nothing's good—you praise God then because you know *God is still God* at midnight. That's the only reason you can praise Him in the darkness. You praise Him then because you know that He's Lord of both daylight and midnight.

You know that these times of darkness are coming your way only because they passed through His fingers first. If God allowed it, He had to first okay it before it could happen to you. He's the almighty God and can stop whatever He wants stopped, so He must have wanted to let it through. And if He wanted to let it through, He wanted to let it through for a reason.

LINKED TO THE SPIRITUAL REALM AND ETERNITY

By singing and praying and praising God at midnight, Paul and Silas were establishing and making connection with the unseen by means of the seen. They entered the invisible by means of praise and worship—which is the fundamental mechanism by which God has given us, His children, the ability to link our lives with the spiritual realm and with eternity.

God is the invisible God. He can't be seen. And the spiritual realm can't be seen either—that's why it is a spiritual realm. But

God has given us a connection to it, which is our praise and adoration and worship.

Worship is how you deliberately "seek the things that are above, where Christ is, seated at the right hand of God"; it's the means by which you "set your minds on things that are above, not on things that are on earth" (Colossians 3:1–2).

Finding the Words

What exactly do you say when you want to worship God at midnight?

You can't talk to Him about what you don't know. You have to fall back on what you *do* know. You have to focus on what you know is true about God.

Sometimes you need somebody to help you praise God at midnight. When you want to worship Him in the darkness but don't know what to say—because you're in too much agony or too much confusion—just open up your Bible to the book of Psalms, and let David's words be the words you use. Those words have the depth you're looking for to praise God at midnight.

When I was a boy, my father bought me a standing punching bag in the shape of a clown. It was big at the bottom and narrow at the top. I could slap and slam that clown and knock it in any direction, but it would always bounce back. I'd beat the death out of it, but it would never stay down. Why? Because the bottom of it was weighted on the inside. And that deep-down weight on the inside overruled what was happening to it on the outside.

That's the way it can be with us. What's on the inside—the things you know for sure about God—can override the difficulty of the trials and circumstances we're experiencing on the outside. The voice of deep experience overflows into words of worship.

SOMETHING HAPPENS

When Paul and Silas worshiped God in the darkness, it wasn't just out of obedience to duty. They praised God because it did something for them.

When you sing to God and praise Him at midnight, something happens. When you praise God when you don't feel like praising Him, when you glorify Him when there doesn't seem to be anything to glorify Him for, there's a profound effect.

It brings about three alterations in particular: Worshiping God in the darkness will change you; it will change your circumstances; and it will change others.

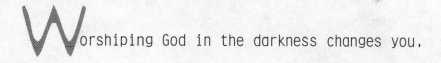

Worshiping God in the darkness changes you.

CHANGING YOU

First, worshiping God in the darkness changes *you*.

When you're suffering and you get your praise on, it lifts your soul out of your situation.

You can see this happening throughout the Psalms. Not all of them are happy psalms. A lot of them are miserable psalms, psalms of struggle, psalms of stress, psalms of danger. The psalmists admit these difficulties. But then, as they begin praising God, they bounce back to bless the Lord.

You may look back to the time when you were saved and recall how this came about at a time when you were in trouble. One reason you decided you needed Christ back then was that things were not going well for you. God used your misery to draw you near to Him, and you came to believe in Jesus Christ for your salvation.

If the Lord first met you when you were in trouble back then and drew you near to Himself, He can surely use your trouble a second time to bring you even closer.

CHANGING YOUR SITUATION

Worshiping God in the dark not only changes you, but can also alter your situation.

Or maybe a better way to explain it is that worshiping God changes you *so that* God in His wisdom is ready and free to change your circumstances.

As you know from Paul and Silas's story, the change in their situation was quick and dramatic: "And suddenly there was a great earthquake, so that the foundations of the prison were shaken. And immediately all the doors were opened, and everyone's bonds were unfastened" (Acts 16:26).

This change came "suddenly"—out of nowhere, unexpectedly, in an unpredictable way. All Paul and Silas did was get into the worship zone, and their world started shaking. A tremor swept through the very foundations of the prison—the thing on which the prison was built. Men can build a prison, but they don't make the ground beneath it; that's God's territory, and He can make it shake.

God Controls the Foundation

No matter how many demons are controlling the prison you find yourself in, God Himself controls the foundations. He made the ground on which your circumstances are built. And He can make it all tremble. He can make the doors fly open and the chains fall off.

Paul and Silas did not have the physical keys to unlock them, but they had the spiritual keys of prayer and praise, and that was enough to trigger a change.

When the hour of midnight comes into your life, God wants to stretch your spiritual stamina while shrinking your self-dependency. He wants to stretch your ability to trust Him when things are tough by severely limiting or even eliminating what you can do by yourself. Then you find yourself saying, "There's no way out of this one." He wants you in the position of being unable to free yourself from your circumstances so that He can be the One who changes those circumstances for you as you worship Him in the dark.

When it's God's earthquake that shakes the foundations and opens the doors and loosens the chains, nobody but God gets the credit. Nobody except God gets the glory.

When you get your praise on and you get God's attention, He responds—especially at midnight. Then you'll see and experience God at a deeper level than you ever thought possible in the daylight, when you can see your own way and can write your own directions.

Changing Others

A third thing that happens when you worship in the dark is that others are changed.

We read that when Paul and Silas were singing and praying, "the prisoners were listening to them" (Acts 16:25). They didn't join in, but they were tuning in.

Other people always want to know what you're going to do at midnight. If you say you're a Christian, they want to see exactly what that will look like for you in the darkness.

These other prisoners who heard Paul and Silas sing were in jail too. They were experiencing their own taste of darkness. It was midnight there for everybody. But only two guys there really knew what to do with midnight, and got their praise on. Only two.

But when the quaking came, it didn't just shake the cell where Paul and Silas were. When doors were opening and chains were falling off, it wasn't just for these two guys. It was for every prisoner there: *"All* the doors were opened, and *everyone's* bonds were unfastened" (v. 26).

Paul and Silas's praise was overflow praise—its effects flowed over beyond them and became a blessing to everyone who'd been listening.

PASSING ALONG THE BLESSING

The effects flowed over even into the life of the jailer—and just in time. "When the jailer woke and saw that the prison doors were open, he drew his sword and was about to kill himself, supposing that the prisoners had escaped" (16:27). He was seconds away from suicide. He saw no hope because he knew the Roman authorities would kill him when they realized all the prisoners had escaped on his watch. He knew he had no chance to live.

"But Paul cried with a loud voice, 'Do not harm yourself, for we are all here'" (v. 28). Paul and Silas and the other prisoners likely could have overpowered the jailer or gotten past him and run away to freedom. But Paul knew that the reason we're blessed is to be a blessing to others; the reason we're delivered is to be a deliverer for those around us. If God comes through for you, He expects you to come through for somebody else. So Paul and Silas ministered to the jailer that night, and he and his entire family became believers.

You're hungry for a breakthrough, for a miracle from God—and God wants to know this: When you get yours, when your rescue comes as you struggle in the darkest waters, will you turn the boat around and go and reach for somebody else?

W hen your rescue comes, will you reach for somebody else?

UNANSWERED QUESTIONS

Have you learned to worship God in your darkest hour?

Job was someone who learned that. When his life was shattered, when overwhelming tragedy struck him, "Job arose and tore his robe and shaved his head and fell on the ground and worshiped. And he said, 'Naked I came from my mother's womb, and naked shall I return. The LORD gave, and the LORD has taken away; blessed be the name of the LORD'" (Job 1:20–21).

He still had many unanswered questions that he would soon bring up, but that didn't stop him from worshiping God. When his life had collapsed, when it seemed there was no reason to praise

God, when there was every reason to reject God, Job worshiped. When God's presence was obscured by circumstances, when Job could not detect His presence anywhere, when it looked like God had closed and locked and double-bolted the door, Job still worshiped.

Job worshiped even though in this life he never received God's full explanation for his suffering. Yet even in the midst of that darkness he could say about God, "He knows the way that I take; when he has tried me, I shall come out as gold" (Job 23:10). Job knew there would be an end to this test. God was working him over, and there was a refining purpose to it whose details were unknown to Job, but the trial someday would end. And when it did, when the refinement was over, it would show Job to be the man God wanted him to be.

REAL VERSUS FAKE WORSHIP

Job's worship was real. You see, there's a lot of fake worship going on. A lot of worship is fake and fraudulent—pretending everything is fine when you know it isn't. God knows you're lying, and most other folk suspect it as well. Everything in your life is *not* fine.

Job's worship was honest. And having built the foundation of real worship, he could openly voice his complaint to God, because when you're talking to a friend, you can be honest. His worship was right out front, and he was open with God, appealing to what he knew to be true about Him.

So many times in our dealings with God we put the word *but* in the wrong place. We say, "I know God is good, but the circumstances He's allowed for me are bad." Or, "I know God is in control, but right now I'm not seeing it." You've got to reverse it and say, "My circumstances are bad, but I know God is wise and loving." "Things are going from bad to worse for me, but I know He's watching over it all; it had to pass through His fingers first."

That's why the knowledge of doctrine and theology is important. Theology and doctrine become meaningful when you have to appeal to what you know amid your darkest hours, when what you're going through doesn't make sense. You have to be able to go deep into the truth God has revealed. But if you don't know that truth, you can't use it when it will mean the most.

EVEN WHEN THE HORIZON IS DARK

Habakkuk was someone else in the Scriptures who came to God with real worship in his darkest hour. The book of Habakkuk is short, only three small chapters, because Habakkuk doesn't have time for pleasantries. He breaks out at the very beginning and cries out, "O LORD, how long shall I cry for help, and you will not hear? Or cry to you 'Violence!' and you will not save?" (1:2).

He knew that what he and the people of God were going through was unjust and unfair. It was wrong. Things shouldn't be this way. How long would it last?

God answers him, and the answer is far from comforting. God said that what was about to happen next would be worse for them than what was already happening. Their horizon looked darker than ever.

Habakkuk becomes more confused than before. The more he thinks about it, the worse his head hurts. But in the final verses of the book, Habakkuk worships, and it isn't fake. I'm sure you've heard it often; think carefully about his words again as a perfect example of worship in the dark times:

> Though the fig tree should not blossom,
>> nor fruit be on the vines,
> the produce of the olive fail
>> and the fields yield no food,
> the flock be cut off from the fold
>> and there be no herd in the stalls,
> yet I will rejoice in the LORD;
>> I will take joy in the God of my salvation.
> GOD, the Lord, is my strength;
>> he makes my feet like the deer's;
>> he makes me tread on my high places. (3:17–19)

NOW IS THE TIME

When your circumstances are dark, when the gloom settles over you, it may have the tendency to shut you down and keep you quiet. But if there's ever a time to worship, that's it. Praise and lift Him up in your tears, your pain, your anger, your struggle. Because God is always developing something in the darkroom. He's getting ready to take you through to your highest level of spiritual growth.

God wants you to realize you can trust Him when you can't see Him, smell Him, taste Him, or feel Him. He wants to know whether you trust Him.

And that's why you keep on worshiping.

are YOU proclaiming?

■ When the Lord touches you with resurrection power—when His Spirit breaks through with a renewal of passion and purpose in your life—He wants you to be able to tell it to others. He wants you to be able to open up your mouth about it.

If it's a real breakthrough, then don't let it be a situation where no one knows it except you. Somebody ought to hear it, so it can bring God glory. We've already got far too many secret-agent Christians whose faith is invisible outside their closet.

DON'T HIDE IT

The bleeding woman Jesus healed in Mark 5 couldn't hide in the crowd any longer. She knew a secret, but Jesus didn't want it to remain a secret. When He asked, "Who touched Me?" He wanted to single her out and put her on public display so everyone would discover what God had done in her life.

Don't forget the surrounding context for this miracle. Jesus was hurrying on His way to minister to the dying daughter of Jairus the synagogue official. So when this interruption occurred, when Jesus stopped to address a low-class woman who had touched Him in order to get well, imagine what might have first gone through the mind of this wealthy and influential man before he had the full picture.

He probably wanted to say to her, "Woman, what do you mean coming out of nowhere like this with your wreck of a life? Don't you realize Jesus is coming with *me,* to heal *my* baby girl who's dying this very minute? We don't have time for all your issues. I have my own issue, and I got to Jesus first, so step aside and let us be going. He'll have to deal with you later."

But as this woman related "the whole truth" (5:33) of what had happened to her, Jairus got to hear fresh new evidence of what Jesus is able to do. And Jesus wanted him to hear this. Because Jairus's situation was just about to get worse. His daughter wasn't just dying; she was already dead.

While Jesus "was still speaking" (v. 35) with the healed woman, people came from Jairus's house to report this tragic news about his little girl. When Jesus turned immediately to Jairus and said, "Do not fear, only believe" (v. 36), Jairus had this woman's miraculous testimony ringing in his ears. There really was no reason to fear; there was every reason to believe in Jesus.

The reason you need to testify about your breakthrough from God is that somebody close to you needs to hear what Jesus can do. They need to know what Jesus is able to do when things go from bad to worse.

Somebody close to you needs to hear what Jesus can do.

■ ■ ■ ■ ■ ■ ■ ■ ■ ■ ■

So my final question for you in this book is this: Are you ready to share with others the truth of what the Lord has done for you?

AMBASSADORS FROM ANOTHER COUNTRY

So many Christians have a hard time sharing the truth about the Lord's work in their lives. And when that's the case, when He's getting no glory from it, God has good reason to hold back from doing more for us.

Why do we struggle so much in this arena? Why are we hesitant to speak out?

A big reason is that we've lost our eternal perspective. The Bible says "we are ambassadors for Christ, God making his appeal through us" (2 Corinthians 5:20). Ambassadors serve in a foreign land that isn't their home. They serve for a temporary time away from home. They're to live in this place where they're assigned, and they have to learn the language and customs of the land, but they're never to belong there or forget where they really belong. They're here not to settle down, but to carry out a mission from their homeland.

The Bible says, "Our citizenship is in heaven" (Philippians 3:20). It teaches that we're "strangers and exiles" in this world (Hebrews 11:13). But too many of us have made this world feel too comfortable. Though we're in a foreign land, we've embraced it as home. We've fallen in love with this country and don't ever want to leave. But the moment an ambassador calls the foreign country home, he's become a traitor, because that's *not* his home. It's the place where he's to carry out his mission from his real home.

When God saved you, He left you here and didn't immediately

take you to heaven because He has a mission for you in this location. He has a divine reason for placing you here. You're His ambassador, representing heaven itself, where your true citizenship is. But what good is an ambassador who doesn't represent the homeland?

JESUS IS THE KEY

As the Lord's ambassadors here, what is our message supposed to be about?

Let me tell you what it *isn't* about. It isn't about what church can do for you. And it isn't even about who God is. What it *is* about is Jesus Christ. The test of your passion is your witness to the gospel of Jesus Christ, not your belief in God.

This distinction becomes clear when we evaluate the kind of responses those things draw from nonbelievers in the world. You can go to church all you want and let everybody know it, but that will seldom get you in trouble. You can tell everyone you believe in God, but that will seldom cause any discomfort for you. You can say grace at mealtime in public, but that will seldom cost you anything except a trace of awkwardness now and then.

Sports champions and entertainers can get on TV and give thanks to God for their performance and their abilities and their breaks, and nobody really minds. People don't mind God-talk because it's general and vague. And anyway, everybody has their own idea about who God is.

But what gets you in real trouble is Jesus Christ. That's what riles people. God isn't a problem to them; Jesus is the problem.

a lot of us will talk about God so we don't have to bring up Jesus.

■ ■ ■ ■ ■ ■ ■ ■ ■ ■ ■ ■

Jesus knew it would be this way for us. He said, "Blessed are you when others revile you and persecute you and utter all kinds of evil against you falsely *on my account*" (Matthew 5:11). It's Jesus who's supposed to be the focal point in your testimony. And when He is, you can expect a negative reaction. When we sense that, however, a lot of us will talk about God so we don't have to bring up Jesus.

Hardly anybody will ever put you down for talking about God. Satan doesn't mind that, because he knows that nobody ever gets saved by believing in God. Nobody goes to heaven just by believing in God. Only by the name of Jesus is anybody delivered from condemnation for their sins. "And there is salvation in no one else, for there is no other name under heaven given among men by which we must be saved" (Acts 4:12).

That's why, in your witnessing, talking about God is never enough, though it may keep you safe from the persecution that comes from mentioning Jesus.

MENTIONING JESUS

I was once invited to come to a city council meeting and open it with prayer. The mayor's letter included the request that I make no mention of Jesus because of the variety of religious beliefs (or lack thereof) held by those who would be in attendance.

Isn't it interesting how Muslims are not asked to avoid mentioning Mohammed. I don't hear Buddhists being requested not to refer to Buddha. Other religious groups are not instructed to ignore their leaders. It's only Jesus Christ that the world is opposed to.

I went to that council meeting, and after I was introduced as the one who would be opening the meeting in prayer, I spoke to this effect:

"Shall we pray?

"Heavenly Father, I want to thank You for the opportunity to pray for the city council's meeting today, as they come to discuss the issues of significance related to our city. I trust that they really do want You to be involved, and that they really do want me to reach You with this prayer.

"You've already told me that there's only one Mediator between God and man, and that is the man Christ Jesus. So I can't do what they've asked me to do without doing it through Jesus Christ.

"First of all, I want to thank You for creating the city council. And according to Colossians 1, everything that was made was made by Jesus Christ, so I have to thank Jesus that the city council is even here.

"I want to thank You for creating government because government is a divine institution, according to the apostle Paul in Romans chapter 13. And Paul is the one who met Jesus on the Damascus road.

"And now, heavenly Father, if there are any city council people here today who do not understand that Jesus was born of a virgin, lived a perfect life, died a substitutionary death, bodily arose from the dead, and is physically coming back again, would You explain that to them sometime today? And bless their decision making. In Jesus' name, amen."

If they didn't want to hear about Jesus, they shouldn't have invited me.

PASSION COMPELS EXPRESSION

You can't help but talk about Jesus if you're truly passionate about Him, because whatever we're passionate about, we talk about. Passion compels expression.

If you go day in and day out, week in and week out, year in and year out having very little to say to anyone about Jesus, there's a reason. His importance in your life hasn't yet reached the level of passion. Because if He had, you'd be talking about Him.

There's no greater message than the good news of Jesus Christ. There's no message more spectacular than the gospel. You can't beat it. The good news that God forgives the sin of sinners and imparts to them the gift of eternal life when they place their faith in Christ alone—that's the message God uses by His Spirit to resurrect a person from spiritual death to spiritual life. And God has invited us to be passionate about it because we're passionate about Him.

When you've got news this hot, you talk about it with a confidence better known as boldness. It's the courage to speak openly and frankly about Jesus.

DESPERATELY NEEDED:
BOLDLY WITNESSING CHRISTIANS

We're in desperate need today for passionate Christians who are bold, who don't want to apologize, who are tired of being secret-agent

Christians, who want to be clearly marked and defined as Christians by their holy boldness.

You can be bold in speaking about Jesus if you know what Jesus can do. And you know what He can do because it's happened to you, and you've seen it happen to others.

Now, if you *don't* know that Jesus can save a man or a woman and give them eternal life, if you *don't* know that His death brings God's forgiveness for them and can change their life forever—if you don't really know this, then don't say anything. But if you've been with Jesus yourself and been forgiven and transformed, and if you've seen it happen to other people as well, then you truly have something to talk about.

Y

ou can be bold in speaking about Jesus if you know what Jesus can do.

■ ■ ■ ■ ■ ■ ■ ■ ■ ■ ■ ■

A BOLDNESS EXAMPLE

Acts 4:13 talks about "the boldness of Peter and John." They had just healed a man who had been lame since birth. They said to this man, "In the name of Jesus Christ of Nazareth, rise up and walk!" (Acts 3:6), and he rose up and walked.

A crowd gathered, and Peter explained to them how "the faith that is through Jesus has given the man this perfect health in the presence of you all" (v. 16). Peter proclaimed Jesus as "the Holy and Righteous One" and "the Author of life" (vv. 14–15) and as the

One whom God the Father sent to suffer and die for our sins and to be raised from the dead.

This got lots of attention from the religious authorities. And they didn't like what they heard. As Peter and John "were speaking to the people, the priests and the captain of the temple and the Sadducees came upon them, greatly annoyed because they were teaching the people and proclaiming in Jesus the resurrection from the dead" (4:1–2). They arrested Peter and John and brought them before the high priest for questioning in regard to this lame man they had healed.

In that setting, Peter was "filled with the Holy Spirit" (v. 8) as he boldly proclaimed Jesus again:

"Let it be known to all of you and to all the people of Israel that by the name of Jesus Christ of Nazareth, whom you crucified, whom God raised from the dead—by him this man is standing before you well. This Jesus is the stone that was rejected by you, the builders, which has become the cornerstone." (4:10–11)

Notice what then went through the minds of the authorities: "Now when they saw the boldness of Peter and John, and perceived that they were uneducated, common men, they were astonished. And they recognized that they had been with Jesus" (v. 13).

They recognized that Peter and John were unlearned and untrained. No Bible college, no seminary. They had no degrees framed and hanging on their walls. They had no theological libraries inside their homes. How could such men be so bold and authoritative in speaking about God?

But something else was also obvious about Peter and John: "They had been with Jesus." These disciples had spent three years with Jesus Christ, walking with Him, talking with Him, interacting with Him, and even during those three years they hadn't got everything right. It wasn't till they saw Him after the resurrection that it really began to make sense for them.

And now it was all paying off. Their intimacy with Christ, their personal knowledge of Christ, created a passion that compelled expression.

YOU CAN BE BOLD

So never think you can't be a bold witness for Christ because you haven't been to seminary or Bible college. Don't say you can't be confident in your testimony for Jesus because you don't have a theological library. Peter and John's only qualification was that they had been with Jesus, and it's all we need as well.

Now, if you *haven't* been with Jesus, I understand. But if you know He saved you, forgave you, and granted you the gift of eternal life, then it's time you got around to being a witness for Him. If you have been with Jesus personally, if He has stepped into your life and redeemed you, that's the only qualification you need to speak with confidence.

Peter and John were ordinary men with extraordinary power because they had been with Jesus and recognized what He could accomplish. They had just seen the power of His name at work in the life of this lame man, and they knew what the name of Jesus had power to do. When you see the Lord change a life like that—including your own—then other people ought to know about it.

W hen something is spectacular, you talk about it.

■ ■ ■ ■ ■ ■ ■ ■ ■ ■ ■ ■

What the Lord does in human lives is spectacular—and when something is spectacular, you talk about it. When you see God take a broken, depraved sinner and pull him up out of the jaws of hell and place him in the Kingdom of God—that's something to talk about. But many of us would far rather talk about the big play we saw in the game on TV last night than talk about the Savior. We'd rather talk about things that have no eternal value at all.

INTENSE OPPOSITION

As Peter and John kept on boldly proclaiming Jesus, the opposition only intensified. The authorities strictly warned these apostles "not to speak or teach at all in the name of Jesus" (Acts 4:18).

Satan's goal back then was just what it is now: He wants every believer to keep quiet about Jesus so the good news doesn't spread any further. He doesn't want it to go anywhere.

This warning from the authorities didn't phase Peter and John. Right on the spot they responded, "We cannot but speak of what we have seen and heard" (v. 20). There was no way they could mute their witness; there was no way they could be silent about the only message that gives men and women eternal life. There was no way they could hold back from talking about the Savior of the world who loved them and died for them and rose from the dead.

So the authorities "further threatened them" and sent them out of their presence.

PRAY FOR BOLDNESS

After their release from jail, Peter and John "went to their friends and reported what the chief priests and the elders had said to them" (Acts 4:23). Did these believers wilt and wither under this warning from the authorities? Did they lose their boldness? Did they decide it was wise to lie low for a while?

No, they got together and prayed—for *more* boldness. "They lifted their voices together to God" (v. 24) with this request: "And now, Lord, look upon their threats and grant to your servants to continue to speak your word *with all boldness*" (v. 29).

When they faced opposition, the early church didn't call a political meeting and pass around recall petitions against the authorities. No, they met together to defeat the enemy with prayer. These New Testament believers recognized that prayer was their connection with God's power and holy boldness.

If you're lacking at all in confidence and boldness—go into God's presence and ask Him for it. Go into God's presence and remind yourself of who you're representing as an ambassador in this world.

Come together with other believers as the family of God in one accord and pray for boldness. Ask for God's help to not keep quiet. Because you know what we so often tend to do: If we witness for Jesus and receive one insult in response, one rejection, one slammed door—then we decide we won't say anything to anybody ever again about Him.

All Under God's Control

In their prayer in Acts 4, those early believers acknowledged to God that when the authorities had opposed Jesus and crucified Him, they were doing "whatever your hand and your plan had predestined to take place" (4:28). That's important to remember. Even when sinners are working against us, they're *not* out from under the control and the plan of God. Even when they did away with Jesus, they were only accomplishing God's predetermined purpose.

When you or I are rejected for representing Jesus, we're never more in the will of God than we are right then. And one day the unbelievers who have rejected your message and who have rejected the Holy Spirit's witness will have to stand before God, and they will stand there legitimately condemned.

So understand completely that as we give men and women the opportunity to make a decision for Jesus Christ, any rejection of that message is not outside God's control.

Now Is the Time

Those early believers prayed for boldness—and God immediately answered. "And when they had prayed, the place in which they were gathered together was shaken, and they were all filled with the Holy Spirit and continued to speak the word of God with boldness" (4:31). God showed up, and His presence was unmistakable.

And God will show up for us as well. Boldness in our witness is His gift to us through the Holy Spirit. We need to seek it and then to live it out. That boldness can be ours because we're representing God. That boldness can be ours because it's the message that saves.

That boldness can be ours because our message is the truth. It can be ours because we have the power of the Holy Spirit.

So—who are you going to talk with today or tomorrow? Who are you going to pray about and ask God to guide you in presenting to them the gospel? Who are you going to lovingly confront?

Now is the time.

Just pray and say, "Lord, here I am—an empty vessel. I invite You to fill me. I give You permission to create an opportunity for me to speak on behalf of Jesus Christ. I don't know much, but I ask You to help me communicate the little I do know in the best way I can."

And this is what will happen to you: As you become a bolder witness for Jesus Christ, you'll see His resurrection power working in your life as you've never seen Him before. You'll sense a passion for Him. The miracle of His renewal will be a living reality for you.

You'll feel like dancing…because those once dry bones will be dry no longer.

a path for Dancing

■ In this book we've looked at some tough questions about a few probing and personal matters. Our reason for doing so is that we want to be ready for the Holy Spirit to blow His fresh, revitalizing power into our lives. We want to expand our capacity to grasp all that God wants to accomplish for us in the way of restoration and renewal. We want to be enabled to hear God's voice of authority and sense His touch of healing and strength, so that dry bones can live again.

As you've explored these questions and examined your life from various angles, I trust that the Holy Spirit has been speaking to your heart and your mind, letting you know the concerns or the issues in your life that He most wants to address at this time, and the active responses and decisions that He wants you to make. God isn't interested in having you read this book merely to accumulate additional knowledge. He has something for you to actually *do*— and He's at work to impart to you the spiritual conviction and comprehension to know what that something is, so you can obey Him and step forth out of dryness and into the miracle of a resurrection life filled with passion and celebration.

A Matter of His Love

When the Lord Jesus spoke to the seven churches in the book of Revelation, and revealed to those people His particular issues and concerns for their lives, He often used a certain word as He wrapped His message up for each of them. And that word is *repent.*

And Jesus even told them (and us) *why* it is that He used this word: "Those whom I love, I reprove and discipline, so be zealous and repent" (Revelation 3:19). You see, it's a *love* issue—a matter of His love for us. Out of that great love, He lets us know what exactly it is we need to change. Then it's our responsibility to "be zealous and repent."

Now the use of that word *repent* presupposes something. Because the last time I checked, there's only one thing you repent of—and that's sin. So when you let any other pursuit get in the way of your pursuit of God, or you look to anything else to provide what only God can give you, or you turn to anyone or anything except God to fill the emptiness and to satisfy the thirst in your life—that, my friend, is sin. It's idolatry. And it's what the Lord wants you to repent of.

To repent means to change your thinking, to alter your mindset, so you can reverse your direction. It all starts with the mind. You've got to mentally acknowledge the truth. You've got to tell yourself the truth—and you've got to mean it when you say it. No matter how many worship songs you sing, no matter how often you take communion, no matter how many inspiring books you read or how many prayers you pray; repentance doesn't really happen until you *change your thinking* about where your life has been headed, and then turn yourself around.

Repentance isn't merely seeing your faults and then shrugging them off by thinking that sooner or later it will all work out. And repentance most emphatically is not looking over at your neighbor and recognizing what he or she is doing wrong. Repentance is looking only at yourself and making the conscious decision that says, "I'm going the wrong way; I need to turn around, and I *will* turn—immediately."

THE TURNAROUND

Imagine you're driving down the freeway and you suddenly realize you're going the wrong way. You're heading south when you need to be traveling north. What do you do?

It's simple. You start looking for the next exit. Why? Because the first chance you get, you're getting off that highway. You've consciously decided, *I'm going the wrong way,* and you've made up your mind to do something about it.

So when you reach that next off-ramp, you take it. But that's not enough. You also have to cross back over the freeway on the overpass, then take the on-ramp to enter the correct lanes to start traveling in the right direction.

That's what true repentance is like. The off-ramp we take is like our moment of confession. We acknowledge we've been traveling the wrong way by hitting the brakes and exiting that road.

The overpass is God's grace—because for all who genuinely confess their sin, God connects us with a bridge of grace that takes us where we need to go.

And the on-ramp represents restoration. You do what it takes to get moving in the right direction, and to make progress toward your life's true destination.

It's the pathway God designed for you, and you can run down it with freedom and exhilaration. In fact, you can dance down that pathway. There'll be no standing still along that course, no standing still, because that would bring only staleness and stagnation. Instead it's a path where we're free to keep moving onward, to keep making forward progress.

CLINGING TO HIS PROMISE

What is it that God has spoken to you about as you've been reading this book?

What has He brought to your mental attention? What is it that He has caused to tug at your heart? What has He shown that represents a wrong direction for you?

Whatever it is, make the decision to turn around. Take the off-ramp of confession, cross over on the overpass of His grace, and take the on-ramp of restoration to live your life in the way God intended and to move forward in the direction He's laid out for you.

Remember again the Lord's words to His people in the book of Revelation: "Behold, I stand at the door and knock. If anyone hears my voice and opens the door, I will come in to him and eat with him, and he with me" (3:20). He's knocking at the door of your life because He wants to come in and be involved in changing things there.

Now normally if our house is a mess and some special person arrives for a visit and knocks at our door, our tendency is to call out, "Just a minute," while we scramble to clean things up a bit. But with Jesus, there's no reason for delay. He already knows how messy the situation is inside. He's already seen all the rooms. He already knows all the confusion and clutter in our personal life and in our family and even in our church. And He's knocking at the door because He wants to come inside and bring about a transformation, a renewal, a resurrection miracle.

He stands and knocks, but that door must be opened from the inside. Our Savior is a gentleman and will not force His way into your heart or your home or your church. But by knocking He will assuredly reveal His presence and His desire to come in and take over. And all you have to do is open that door to Him.

Then you'll see with your own eyes how God will do for you that which you sensed is impossible. The living and mighty God of the impossible will invade your dryness and your discouragement and even your hopelessness. Like those bones in Ezekiel's valley, He'll bring together that which is scattered in disarray. The winds of the His Holy Spirit will blow, and suddenly there'll be life— energy and exuberance and vivacity and purpose and fulfillment—where life was lacking before.

Trust Him for this. Draw near to the everlasting God and experience His faithfulness as never before. Draw near enough to hear His promise for you, and then cling to it: "I will put my Spirit within you, and you shall live…. Then you shall know that I am the LORD; I have spoken, and I will do it, declares the LORD" (Ezekiel 37:14).

Amen.

study &
Discussion
Guide

....

Use these questions to help you think more carefully about the content and message of this book and apply it to your life.

PART I: FROM DEADNESS TO DANCING

Chapter 1: Down in the Valley

Purpose
(a) To become thoroughly familiar with the vision God gave to the prophet Ezekiel of the valley filled with dry bones (Ezekiel 37), and (b) to begin to recognize and appreciate the message from God that this vision contains for your own life.

Questions for Study, Discussion, and Application

1. In what ways, if any, have you sensed personal need of miraculous spiritual renewal and restoration from God in your life or in your family's life or in your church's life?

2. In what ways, if any, have you felt that a needed renewal in your life or in your family's life or in your church's life just

isn't possible? What degree of hopelessness have you known in this regard?

3. What are you expecting and trusting God to do in this situation?

4. What would you expect to see if God were to grant you a personal vision that depicted the true reality...

   a) of your own spiritual condition?

   b) of your family's spiritual condition?

c) of your church's spiritual condition?

d) of your nation's spiritual condition?

5. From Ezekiel 37, what strikes you most about the vision God gave Ezekiel of the valley filled with dry bones? What do you see as the most important aspects of that vision?

Scripture Passages to Explore
The vision of the valley of dry bones—Ezekiel 37:1–14
Also: Ezekiel 3:22–23; 8:4; Hebrews 4:12

Chapter 2: There's a Reason for This

Purpose
To thoroughly grasp the concept that spiritual dryness is caused by distance from God, which is caused by disobedience.

Questions for Study, Discussion, and Application

1. In the past, what have you most often considered to be the reason for any spiritual dryness you or other believers have experienced?

2. Have you known an extensive period of spiritual dryness in your life? If so, how long did it last?

3. Describe what evidence you see—in your own life or in the lives of other believers you know—of the truth of this

statement: "Disobedience creates distance, and distance creates dryness."

4. What is more prevalent in your life—spiritual dryness or spiritual rejoicing?

5. How trustworthy is your self-assessment of your spirituality?

6. What things are most likely to become idols in your life, in competition with God?

7. How warm is your love affair with God at this time?

8. Remember to pray this prayer: "Holy Spirit, as I read through these pages, give me the specific application for me. I need to hear Your voice. Show me what You want me to do."

Scripture Passages to Explore
Idolatry: Ezekiel 6:9; 14:5; 20:16; 36:17–18
Also: Matthew 6:24; 11:30; Philippians 4:4; 1 John 5:3; Revelation 2:4; 3:17–19

Chapter 3: When the Spirit's Wind Blows

Purpose

To comprehend in a new way the essential role of the Holy Spirit in your Christian life.

Questions for Study, Discussion, and Application

1. Why exactly do you need the Holy Spirit in your life? How is your need of Him demonstrated in your prayer life in a normal day?

2. How much of the Holy Spirit's power are you experiencing in a typical day?

3. What is your understanding of the New Covenant? What difference does this covenant make in our lives?

4. In what aspects of your life do you face the greatest temptation to be "earthbound" in your thinking, instead of having a heavenly and godly perspective?

5. When was the last time you felt the Holy Spirit blowing fresh vitality into your life?

6. What do you most want to change in your life through the "updraft" of the Holy Spirit?

Scripture Passages to Explore

Promise of the Spirit: Ezekiel 11:19–20; 18:31–32; 36:25–27

New Covenant: Jeremiah 31:31–34; Matthew 26:28; Hebrews 8:7–13; 12:24

Also: Genesis 2:7; Nehemiah 8:10; Zechariah 4:6; John 7:38–39; 10:10; Acts 1:8; 2 Corinthians 3:6; Hebrews 4:12

Chapter 4: Your Resurrection

Purpose

To ponder the stirring reality that Jesus Christ Himself *is* the resurrection in the present reality of our lives.

Questions for Study, Discussion, and Application

1. What does it truly mean to you that you possess the gift of life from Jesus Christ? And what do you believe He wants most for you to do with this gift at this moment?

2. What does it truly mean to you that you possess the gift of liberty from Jesus Christ? And what do you believe He wants most for you to do with this gift at this moment?

3. What does it truly mean to you that you possess the gift of love from Jesus Christ? And what do you believe He wants most for you to do with this gift at this moment?

Scripture Passages to Explore

Jesus is the resurrection: John 11:1–44

Also: Luke 4:18; John 8:36; 12:2; Revelation 3:20

PART II: Deepening Your Spiritual Passion

Chapter 5: Are You Hungry?

Purpose

To intensify your spiritual appetite for experiencing God.

Questions for Study, Discussion, and Application

1. To what degree can you identify with the professional athlete who said he couldn't find the time to have devotions? To what extent can you identify with the athlete who spoke of the inability to persuade God in prayer to remove a stronghold from his life?

2. How would you describe the intensity of your hunger for God at this time in your life?

3. In what ways can you identify with Zacchaeus and how he acted toward Jesus?

4. Have you ever been content to merely be a part of the "Jesus Fan Club," instead of truly hungering for what Jesus offers?

5. Zacchaeus climbed a sycamore tree to catch a better view of Jesus. What do you need to do to see Jesus more clearly?

6. What spiritual "junk food" have you been letting yourself have, instead of solid spiritual food from Jesus?

7. What can you do now to increase your spiritual capacity for
   the Lord?

Scripture Passages to Explore
Zacchaeus and Jesus: Luke 19:1–10
Also: Matthew 5:6

Chapter 6: Are You Asking?

Purpose
To quicken your readiness to request from God everything you need for a life of spiritual passion.

Questions for Study, Discussion, and Application

1. At what times have you felt that God was truly all you had? What was that experience like?

2. How is your communication with God these days? Is it meaningful and strong?

3. What does it mean to you, in a practical way, to "consciously bring God to bear on everything?" What would this look like in your life?

4. What is it like for you to hear God's voice through your meditation in the Scriptures? What does this require of you?

5. What illumination do you need to ask for from God at this time in your life? What clarity and guidance do you need?

6. Moses asked God to show him His glory. In what ways is that your prayer as well?

Scripture Passages to Explore

Moses' prayer: Exodus 33:7–23

Also: Job 42:5; Matthew 17:1–8; John 15:15; 1 Thessalonians 5:17

Chapter 7: Are You Drawing Near?

Purpose

To encourage you to accept the Lord's invitation to draw nearer and nearer to Himself.

Questions for Study, Discussion, and Application

1. What are the issues in your life at this time that cause you to turn in desperation to the Lord?

2. What impressed you most about the faith of the woman in Mark 5 who approached Jesus from behind to touch Him?

3. How have you seen in your life that grace is greater than law?

4. In Mark 5, Jesus had questions for His disciples and for the crowds. What questions is Jesus asking you today?

5. God says in Jeremiah 9:24, "Let him who boasts boast in this, that he understands and knows me." Is this something you can boast of?

Scripture Passages to Explore

The bleeding woman and Jesus: Mark 5:21–34

Also: Leviticus 15:25–31; Jeremiah 9:23–24; John 1:17

Chapter 8: Are You Paying the Price?

Purpose

To awaken you to the reality of the specific sacrifices the Lord wants you to make as you follow and obey Him.

Questions for Study, Discussion, and Application

1. Why does God require sacrifices from us? And in your thinking, how does this fit with the concept of being saved by grace instead of by works?

2. What major tests has God brought into your life? In what ways do you sense that He's testing you now?

3. God asked Abraham to give up the most precious thing in his life, his son Isaac. What are the most precious things in your life? Does God have full ownership of them, as far as your heart's deepest affections are concerned?

4. How is God testing and expanding your faith at this time in your life? What are you trusting Him for in a deeper and stronger way?

5. What things is God doing or allowing in your life at this time that make little or no sense to you? How does this test your faith in Him?

6. What, if anything, is God asking you to "take the knife to"?

Scripture Passages to Explore

Abraham and Isaac: Genesis 21:12; 22:1–19; Hebrews 11:17–19

Also: 2 Samuel 24:24; Isaiah 55:8–9; Matthew 6:33; Luke 14:26; John 21:15

Chapter 9: Are You Enduring?

Purpose

To further energize your ability to steadfastly endure all that God gives you to endure as you faithfully serve Him and wait for Him.

Questions for Study, Discussion, and Application

1. At what times have you felt that God has given you more difficulty than you can bear? How has this turned you in dependence to Him?

2. When, if ever, have you felt abandoned by God? How did God bring you back into a sense of His presence?

3. When is it hardest for you to consciously choose to remember God?

4. What are the strongest ways in your past in which God has demonstrated His grace to you?

5. How have you sensed God giving you strength when you were thoroughly weary?

6. How have you sensed the Spirit's "updraft" so that spiritually you can "mount up with wings" like an eagle?

7. How have you sensed a burst of "second wind" from the Lord, enabling you to go on when the going was tough?

8. In what arenas of life do you need fresh new energy? Are you asking and trusting God for this?

Scripture Passages to Explore
Psalm 42; 73; Isaiah 40:27–31
Also: Psalm 27:14; 1 Corinthians 10:13; Philippians 3:10; 1 Peter 4:12–13

Chapter 10: Are You Worshiping?

Purpose
To fortify your ability to wholeheartedly worship the Lord, even in times of darkness.

Questions for Study, Discussion, and Application

1. What does worship mean to you? What does it actually involve on your part? And what makes worship real instead of fake?

2. When have you felt that you were experiencing a "midnight" in your life? Were you able to praise God and pray to Him in this time?

3. Why does God expect us to worship Him in our darkest hours?

4. What convinces you that God has full control over the details of your life, even when you face the worst difficulties?

5. When you've worshiped God in times of darkness, how have you seen Him bring about changes in yourself, in your circumstances, or in the lives of those around you?

Scripture Passages to Explore

Paul and Silas in prison: Acts 16:16–40

Job's worship: Job 1:20–21; 23:10

Habakkuk's worship: Habakkuk 1:2; 3:17–19

Also: John 16:33; 2 Corinthians 4:8; Philippians 4:4; Colossians 3:1–2

Chapter 11: Are You Proclaiming?

Purpose
To help you deepen your commitment to be a faithful witness to Jesus Christ in the world around you.

Questions for Study, Discussion, and Application

1. What does it mean to you to bring God glory through your witness for Jesus Christ?

2. Is it hard for you to witness to Jesus Christ as you talk with unbelievers? If so, what makes it difficult for you?

3. Why does Satan want us to be weak and hesitant in our witness for Jesus Christ?

4. What does it mean to you to be an ambassador for Christ during your life on this earth?

5. Are you praying for the Holy Spirit's boldness in your witness for Jesus Christ?

Scripture Passages to Explore

Ambassadors for Christ: 2 Corinthians 5:20; Philippians 3:20

Peter and John's boldness: Acts 3–4

Also: Matthew 5:11; Hebrews 11:13

Chapter 12: A Path for Dancing

Purpose
To encourage you to take deliberate action in response to what God has taught you through reading this book.

Questions for Study, Discussion, and Application

I. At this time in your life, how would you answer the questions presented in the chapter titles in the second part of this book, as they relate to your relationship with God and your passion for Him:

—Are you hungry?
—Are you asking?
—Are you drawing near?
—Are you paying the price?
—Are you enduring?
—Are you worshiping?
—Are you proclaiming?

2. What does repentance mean to you? What are some examples of repentance before God in your life in the past?

3. Concerning the present state of your soul and your spiritual life, what is it that God has spoken most to you about as

you've been reading this book? What has He brought to your attention or burdened your heart with? What has He shown that represents a wrong direction for you?

4. What repentance do you need to follow through with at this time?

5. What do you need to trust God for at this time?

6. How exactly has reading this book been a help for you?

Scripture Passages to Explore

Repentance: Job 42:5–6; Acts 8:22; Revelation 2–3

THE GOOD SHEPHERD

T ony Evans leads us through an examination of Psalm 23 to help us understand that God supplies us with absolutely all that we need.

"Tony Evans is one of the greatest preachers in America today. When he writes, I listen."

—CHUCK COLSON

All of us go through good, bad, and ugly times. God can take all of the experiences of your life and use them to make you unbelievably better at what He's created you for!

JESUS SAID,
"YOU WILL RECEIVE POWER WHEN THE HOLY SPIRIT COMES UPON YOU."

What kind of a difference is the Holy Spirit making in your daily life? Tony Evans provides clear, simple teaching straight from God's Word on how to intimately know the Holy Spirit—His fruit, His power, His guidance—for a victorious life.

Printed in the United States
by Baker & Taylor Publisher Services